Blockchain and Machine Learning for IoT Security

The Internet of Things (IoT) involves physical devices, cars, household appliances, and any other physical appliance equipped with sensors, software, and network connections to gather and communicate data. Nowadays, this technology is embedded in everything from simple smart devices, to wearable equipment, to complex industrial machinery and transportation infrastructures. On the other hand, IoT equipment has been designed without considering security issues. Consequently, there are many challenges in terms of protection against IoT threats, which can lead to distressing situations. In fact, unlike other technological solutions, there are few standards and guidelines governing the protection of IoT technology. Moreover, few users are aware of the risks associated with IoT systems.

Thus, ***Blockchain and Machine Learning for IoT Security*** discusses various recent techniques and solutions related to IoT deployment, especially security and privacy. This book addresses a variety of subjects, including a comprehensive overview of the IoT, and covers in detail the security challenges at each layer by considering how both the architecture and underlying technologies are employed. As acknowledged experts in the field, the authors provide remediation solutions for impaired security, as well as mitigation methods, and offer both prevention and improvement suggestions.

Key Features:

- Offers a unique perspective on IoT security by introducing Machine Learning and Blockchain solutions

- Presents a well-rounded overview of the most recent advances in IoT security and privacy

- Discusses practical solutions and real-world cases for IoT solutions in various areas

- Provides solutions for securing IoT against various threats

- Discusses Blockchain technology as a solution for IoT

This book is designed to provide all the necessary knowledge for young researchers, academics, and industry professionals who want to understand the advantages of artificial intelligence technology, machine learning, data analysis methodology, and Blockchain for securing IoT technologies.

Blockchain and Machine Learning for IoT Security

Edited by

Mourade Azrour, Jamal Mabrouki,
Azidine Guezzaz, and Said Benkirane

CRC Press
Taylor & Francis Group
Boca Raton London New York

CRC Press is an imprint of the
Taylor & Francis Group, an **informa** business

A CHAPMAN & HALL BOOK

First edition published 2024
by CRC Press
2385 NW Executive Center Drive, Suite 320, Boca Raton FL 33431

and by CRC Press
4 Park Square, Milton Park, Abingdon, Oxon, OX14 4RN

CRC Press is an imprint of Taylor & Francis Group, LLC

ISBN: 9781032563442 (hbk)
ISBN: 9781032573014 (pbk)
ISBN: 9781003438779 (ebk)

DOI: 10.1201/9781003438779

Typeset in Minion
by Deanta Global Publishing Services, Chennai, India

Contents

About the Editors

Prof. Mourade Azrour obtained his PhD from the Faculty of Sciences and Techniques, Moulay Ismail University of Meknes, Morocco. He received his MS in Computer and Distributed Systems from the Faculty of Sciences, Ibn Zouhr University, Agadir, Morocco, in 2014. Mourade currently works as a Professor of Computer Sciences at the Department of Computer Science, Faculty of Sciences and Techniques, Moulay Ismail University of Meknes. His research interests include Authentication Protocol, Computer Security, Internet of Things, Smart Systems, Machine Learning, and so on. Mourade is a member of the scientific committee of numerous international conferences. He is also a reviewer of various scientific journals. He has published more than 60 scientific papers and book chapters. Mourade has edited two scientific books *IoT and Smart Devices for Sustainable Environment* and *Advanced Technology for Smart Environment and Energy*. Finally, he has served as guest editor for the journals *EAI Endorsed Transactions on Internet of Things, Tsinghua Science and Technology, Applied Sciences MDPI*, and *Sustainability MDPI*.

Prof. Jamal Mabrouki obtained his PhD in Process and Environmental Engineering at Mohammed V University, Rabat, Morroco, specializing in Artificial Intelligence and Smart Automatic Systems. He completed a BSc in Physics and Chemistry with honors from Hassan II University, Casablanca, Morocco. His research is on intelligent monitoring, control, and management systems, and more particularly on sensing and supervising remote intoxication systems, smart self-supervised systems, and recurrent neural networks. He has published several papers in conferences and indexed journals, most of them related to artificial intelligence systems, the Internet of Things, and big data and mining. Jamal currently works as a Professor of Environment, Energy, and Smart Systems at the Faculty of Science, Mohammed V University. Jamal is a scientific committee member of numerous national and international conferences. He is also a reviewer for *Modeling Earth Systems and Environment, International Journal of Environmental Analytical Chemistry, International Journal of Modeling, Simulation, and Scientific Computing, The Journal of Supercomputing, Energy & Environment*, and *Big Data Mining and Analytics*.

Prof. Azidine Guezzaz obtained his PhD from Ibn Zohr University, Agadir, Morocco, in 2018. He obtained his MSc in Computer and Distributed Systems from the Faculty of Sciences, Ibn Zouhr University in 2013. He is currently an Associate Professor of Computer Science and Mathematics at Cadi Ayyad University, Marrakech, Morocco. His main fields of research interest are Computer Security, Cryptography, Artificial Intelligence, Intrusion Detection, and Smart Cities. He is a member of the scientific and organizing committee of various international conferences. Azidine is a guest editor of special issues of the journals *Tsinghua Science and Technology, Sustainability*, and *EAI Endorsed Transactions on Internet of Things*. He is also an editor of some books and a reviewer of various scientific journals.

Prof. Said Benkirane obtained his BEng in Networks and Telecommunications in 2004 from Institut National des Postes et Télécommunications (INPT), Rabat, Morocco. He obtained his MSc in Computer and Network Engineering in 2006 at the Sidi Mohamed Ben Abdellah University of Fez, and his PhD in Computer Science in 2013 from the Chouaib Doukkali University of El-Jadida, Morocco. He worked as a Professor from 2014 at ESTE Cadi Ayyad University, Marrakech, Morocco. His areas of research are Artificial Intelligence, Multi-Agents, and Systems Security. He also works in various wireless networks (for example, VANET and WSN). He is President of the Robotics and Artificial Intelligence Team in Higher School of Technology Essaouira, Morocco and is also an active reviewer in several high-quality journals.

Contributors

Abdulatif Alabdulatif
Department of Computer Science
Qassim University
Buraydah, Saudi Arabia

Adetayo Olaniyi ADENIRAN
Federal University of
   Technology
Akure, Nigeria

Ahmad El Allaoui
STI Laboratory, IDMS Team
Faculty of Sciences and
   Techniques
Moulay Ismail University of
   Meknes
Errachidia, Morocco

Azidine Guezzaz
Higher School Essaouira
Cadi Ayyad University
Marrakech, Morocco

Aziz Mabrouk
Approximation Problem
   Modeling & Data Science
   Research Team
Abdelmalek Essaadi University
Tetouan, Morocco

Chaimae Hazman
Higher School Essaouira
Cadi Ayyad University
Marrakech, Morocco

Divya Prakash
Department of Computer Science
   and Application
Koneru Lakshmaiah Education
   Foundation
Vaddeswaram, India

Feyisola Olajire AKINSEHINWA
Federal University of Technology
Akure, Nigeria

G. Krishna Mohan
Department of Computer Science
   and Application
Koneru Lakshmaiah Education
   Foundation
Vaddeswaram, India

Ghufran Ahmad Khan
Department of Computer Science
   and Application
Koneru Lakshmaiah Education
   Foundation
Vaddeswaram, India

Hanaa Attou
Higher School Essaouira
Cadi Ayyad University
Marrakech, Morocco

Hasna Hissou
Science and Technology Research
    Structure
Faculty of Science
Chouaïb Doukkali University
El Jadida, Morocco

Jamal Mabrouki
Laboratory of Spectroscopy
Molecular Modelling,
    Materials, Nanomaterial,
    Water and Environment,
    CERNE2D
Mohammed V University
Rabat, Morocco

Kamal Bella
Higher School Essaouira
Cadi Ayyad University
Marrakech, Morocco

M. Preethi
Department of Computer Science
    and Application
Koneru Lakshmaiah Education
    Foundation
Vaddeswaram, India

Mohamed Abdedaime
National School of Business and
    Management
Ibn Tofail University
Kenitra, Morocco

Mouaad Mohy-eddine
Higher School Essaouira
Cadi Ayyad University
Marrakech, Morocco

Mourade Azrour
STI Laboratory
IDMS Team
Moulay Ismail University of Meknes
Errachidia, Morocco

Rafeeq Ahmed
Department of Computer Science
    and Engineering
Koneru Lakshmaiah Education
    Foundation
Vaddeswaram, India

Said Benkirane
Higher School Essaouira
Cadi Ayyad University
Marrakech, Morocco

Samuel Oluwaseyi Olorunfemi
Federal University of Technology
Akure, Nigeria

Sara Amaouche
Higher School Essaouira
Cadi Ayyad University
Marrakech, Morocco

Shaik Yasmin
Department of Computer Science
    and Application
Koneru Lakshmaiah Education
    Foundation
Vaddeswaram, India

Souhayla Dargaoui
STI Laboratory, IDMS Team
Moulay Ismail University of
    Meknes
Errachidia, Morocco

Taushif Anwar
Department of Computer Science
    and Application
Koneru Lakshmaiah Education
    Foundation
Vaddeswaram, India

Zubair Ashraf
Department of Computer
    Engineering & Applications
GLA University
Mathura, Uttar Pradesh, India

Zulfikar Ali Ansari
Department of Computer Science
    and Engineering
Koneru Lakshmaiah Education
    Foundation
Vaddeswaram, India

Google Trend Analysis of Airport Passenger Throughputs: Case Study of Murtala Muhammed International Airport

Adetayo Olaniyi Adeniran, Samuel Oluwaseyi Olorunfemi, Feyisola Olajire Akinsehinwa, and Mourade Azrour

1.1 INTRODUCTION

In Nigeria, air transport has contributed to the Nigerian economy [1], especially in creating direct and indirect jobs. The major contribution to the Nigerian economy by the air transport industry is derived from the international throughputs (passengers and cargoes) in Lagos [2]. According to the data released by the National Bureau of Statistics (NBS), the total number of international passengers who passed through the Nigerian airports was 2,219,146, which was a 57.61% growth rate and the passenger throughputs [3]. From that number, Murtala Muhammed International

DOI: 10.1201/9781003438779-1

Airport (MMIA) recorded 1,595,522 passengers, which was the highest. International airports in Nigeria are either domestic or international. Among all, MMIA was tagged as the busiest airport over the years, and it serves as the hub for connecting flights to many countries [4].

Since the throughput of passengers pressures Lagos Airport, the city plans on increasing infrastructural capacity that will be capable of meeting the needs and demands of international passengers and airlines [5]. With this plan being implemented, other international airlines will be allocated space within the terminal, and that gives opportunities for more airline patronage which enhances significant contribution to the aviation industry and Nigerian economy.

It is pertinent to note that air travel demand modeling and forecasting have generated significant attention among practitioners and academics [6]. Also, development in information technologies such as the Internet of Things (IoT) [7]–[14], Big Data Analytics, Blockchain, Machine Learning [15]–[17], Artificial Intelligence (AI) [18]–[25], Augmented Reality Systems, and Location-based Services, has given birth to a huge amount of big data that are generated by tourists [26]. This data entails mobile device locations, social media mentions, and search query data [27].

In previous years, diverse variables (predictors) have been employed to determine the demand and supply for air travel, passenger departure and arrival, tourist demand, and direct and indirect businesses related to aviation. These were all the major, fashionable, and significant measures [28] which is differentiated with the dynamics of air travel demand.

Furthermore, Kumar and Kashif [29] perceived that the expenditure of air passengers at a destination is usually employed as the demand variable. In recent times, the exploitation of search query data has been increasing, and this is made available through different sources, most especially Google Trends (www.google.com/trends). Pradeep and Rajesh [30] noted that forecasting techniques are suitable for modeling the customers' or users' cycles and processes; Google Trends is among the tools for forecasting. An example of the cycle is the customer journey map for optimizing sales and marketing processes [31]. Since the Internet is predominantly employed by travelers when planning a journey, Choi and Varian [32] perceived that the data available and extracted from Google Trends data regarding destinations can be suitable for predicting actual passengers' visits to that exact destination through a particular airport.

From the above discussions, new possibilities for airport demand forecasting and planning can be made available with big data. Nonetheless, there are some issues concerning how the big data is being captured, searching for big data, analysis and interpretation of big data, sharing of big data, storing of big data, transfer of big data, privacy of big data, and visualization of big data. These issues require new technological approaches, or programs that can reveal hidden (unseen) values from this bigger data [33]. Therefore, one of the programs required to expand the benefit of using big data for airport demand forecasting is Google Trends.

The objective of this study is to determine the suitability of Google Trends for forecasting airport demand in Lagos, Nigeria. From a theoretical standpoint, the contribution of this study to literature is rooted in Google Trends literature and most especially in airport demand forecasting. The analysis provided in this study is relevant for forecasting airport demand in Lagos, with increasing understanding of airport demand and Google Trends.

The adoption of Google Trends is a free approach for demand forecasting based on human behavior in online searches and actions of actual passengers that pass through the airport. It enhances airport management and the aviation industry with the opportunity to accurately and efficiently respond to the airport demand, which could result to improved experiences for the airport users and improved planning for the government and concerned organizations.

The practical relevance of this study for the MMIA is that it will provide a leeway for the government to react efficiently to the airport users' demand, which could result in a better performance of MMIA in Lagos and a significant contribution to the Nigerian economy. The totality of the airport and aviation industry can benefit from this study because new opportunities such as users' behavior and forecasting could be revealed to them regarding the spatial interaction of passengers and airlines, and providing a more robust transport system that could connect the airport.

1.2 EMPIRICAL REVIEW

Because of the current availability of web-based data sources, there has been a natural relationship with air travel demand. Customer feedback via review platforms, search engine traffic, and site traffic are all examples of web-based data sources. This huge data has been used to forecast air travel demand and airport demand [34].

Previous research has primarily relied on surveys or expert judgments. This implies that samples from the entire population were adopted and may not have accurate data on all travelers [35]. The use of big data in relation to aviation throughputs may provide advantages over traditional methods. To start with, there is an increase in data consistency because it is motiveless data based on users' actual activities and behaviors rather than samples, which improves the consideration of all information aspects to provide exact results rather than subjective conclusions as a result of data loss caused by the use of sample data.

Second, because big data on aviation is created by visitors, it improves knowledge about aviation businesses, airport businesses, and airline markets, and is useful for assessing users' desire for airport services [36]. There is a chance that other data sources will be cross-referenced with the big data. This might lead to the establishment of an equilibrium between the demand for and supply of aviation services and products.

The most significant benefit of big data is the capacity to cast data, which is contained in the use of real-time data to explain concurrent online actions prior to a data source, data presentation, and availability [37]. On the other hand, big data is linked to a variety of difficulties [38].

Furthermore, the relevance of the data may fade in a short period of time. For example, if a client (consumer) is no longer at a certain area, it is not relevant to realize that such a consumer is close to a business. The modern world is driven by technology, and technology cannot be effective without real-time data [39]. Real-time data is required to determine when data is no longer relevant for present-day analysis.

Later, the representativeness of huge data becomes a concern, potentially leading to biases in data sampling and sampling techniques. For example, some people use the internet to express their unhappiness with a certain product or a characteristic of a product that the maker may not be aware of. In some cases, the manufacturer may be unsure of the complaint's dynamics. It is important to note that this type of complaint could come from a real customer, but it could also come from a competitor who wants to distract the manufacturers or sabotage a specific brand. Collaboration, as well as the usage of big data, has advantages and disadvantages.

1.3 METHODS

For several years, scholars have attempted to estimate air travel demand and tremendous progress has been made in this area. Despite the many forecasting methodologies, Witt and Witt (2015) stated that those employed in anticipating travel demand are insufficient. Spatial models, time-series models, and econometric models are the most often employed quantitative forecasting methods.

1.3.1 Research Design

Using both deductive and inductive approaches, this study estimated airport demand in the form of passenger throughputs in Murtala Muhammed International Airport (MMIA) using Google Trends. In terms of data sources, quantitative data such as Google Trends and the exact data on embarking and disembarking passengers that made use of MMIA in Lagos were employed. Because it is based on trends and patterns observed by Google Trends, the study is simulated in the form of time-series modeling. This type of study is practical since it just requires historical observations of variables [40].

Finding suitable Google Trends keywords or search phrases is a crucial element of this forecasting study. Both an inductive and a deductive strategy will be employed for this. To begin, the customer journey theory was used to remove search query terms. It examined how strong the relationship is between these terms and the pattern of each search query relating to demand in MMIA. A more conventional inductive technique was employed to analyze Google Trends data. This was accomplished by linking the number of travelers to Google Trends and vice versa using Google Correlate. Based on this, the study identified other search terms and keywords for this field of interest.

1.3.2 Data Collection and Analysis

Secondary data were extracted from Google Trends, and published data on passenger throughputs in MMIA were extracted from the National Bureau of Statistics (NBS) and the Federal Airports Authority of Nigeria (FAAN). This study focused on the calendar years 2004–2021 on passenger demand in MMIA. Data obtained from published reports was filtered, but data obtained from Google Trends using keyword selection was aggregated, and it is of high significance. As stated in the study's theory, the researcher undertaking the study must employ airport-related keywords, obtain search query data, and select appropriate data.

The most difficult aspect is keyword selection. The customer journey theory was utilized to generate the keywords for the first phase of the investigation. For the customer journey's awareness or need phase the keywords were Murtala Muhammed International Airport (MMIA1), Muritala Muhammed International Airport (MMIA2), Murtala Mohammed International Airport (MMIA3), Murtala Muhammed International Airport Lagos (MMIAL), Murtala Muhammed International Airport

Lagos Nigeria (MMIALN), Lagos Airport (LA), Lagos International Airport (LIA), and Airport in Lagos (AiL).

For this study, the keywords with correlation values between r = 0.80 and r = 1.0 may be related to airport demand in MMIA. The data was examined with descriptive and correlation analysis.

1.4 RESULTS AND DISCUSSION

The findings of the data analysis were reported in this section. The actual throughputs of air traveler inflow to Nigeria through MMIA were evaluated, as well as preliminary data from Google Trends, and then a correlation study was given. This study investigated the correlations between search terms for air travelers that pass through MMIA (worldwide) and total passenger throughputs in MMIA over 18 years (2004–2021). The instances of travelers that pass through MMIA in Lagos were investigated. According to Google, the search engine with the highest share improves forecasting of passenger behavior.

1.4.1 Extent to Which Data Provided by Google Trends Are Valuable for Forecasting Passenger Throughputs in MMIA

Regarding the share of Google search for tourist visits in London, the following variables: Murtala Muhammed International Airport (MMIA1), Muritala Muhammed International Airport (MMIA2), Murtala Mohammed International Airport (MMIA3), Murtala Muhammed International Airport Lagos (MMIAL), Murtala Muhammed International Airport Lagos Nigeria (MMIALN), Lagos Airport (LA), Lagos International Airport (LIA), and Airport in Lagos (AiL) were searched using Google trend for planning phase of customer journey as shown in Table 1.1 and Figure 1.1.

Figure 1.1 shows the yearly data of search terms for customer journey keywords. From the trend, it was revealed that three variables (Lagos Airport, Airport in Lagos, and Lagos International Airport) have the highest search scores respectively, therefore air travelers around the world search more of those three queries when planning for a visit to Lagos, Nigeria. This could also be a result of the popularity of Lagos in Nigeria and Africa, being the center of commerce and industrialization. The search queries of "Lagos Airport", "Airport in Lagos", and "Lagos International Airport" come to mind rather than the exact MMIA which is the airport name, hence, it is most suitable for predicting customer journeys to Lagos and Nigeria for any form of trip purpose.

TABLE 1.1 Comparison of search terms for customer journey keywords on a yearly basis

Year	MMIA1	MMIA2	MMIA3	MMIAI	MMIALN	LA	LIA	AiL
Yr 2004	257	82	162	105	226	284	146	191
Yr 2005	58	56	270	172	27	444	62	103
Yr 2006	38	70	69	45	13	674	180	82
Yr 2007	57	190	94	10	21	542	77	76
Yr 2008	30	82	35	16	11	586	138	140
Yr 2009	19	0	49	2	11	650	152	169
Yr 2010	21	74	45	11	6	632	127	142
Yr 2011	49	93	20	12	9	614	160	129
Yr 2012	69	13	31	14	19	718	217	167
Yr 2013	66	12	28	20	2	728	188	188
Yr 2014	73	15	25	15	3	731	188	215
Yr 2015	75	0	12	14	3	754	209	220
Yr 2016	72	22	13	7	2	775	219	216
Yr 2017	81	12	9	9	5	867	211	221
Yr 2018	65	29	10	12	3	922	208	241
Yr 2019	105	29	15	14	3	950	235	235
Yr 2020	102	23	9	21	4	706	248	192
Yr 2021	89	7	8	12	8	688	210	197

Source: Google Trends (2021)

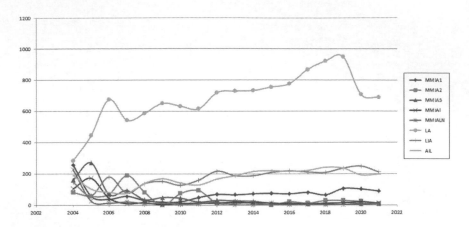

FIGURE 1.1 Trend analysis of customer search terms for international air passenger throughputs in Lagos airport

Regarding the correlation of the Google trend data between the three dominant search queries as shown in Table 1.2, the correlation between the search queries of Lagos Airport and Lagos International Airport, which is 0.724 (p-value 0.000 < 0.01), revealed that there is a positive and significant relationship between the data of search terms of Lagos Airport and Lagos International Airport within the study period. The correlation between the search queries of Lagos Airport and Airport in Lagos is 0.602 (p-value 0.008 > 0.01), which revealed that there is a positive but insignificant relationship between the data of search terms of Lagos Airport and Airport in Lagos. Finally, the correlation between the search queries of Lagos International Airport and Airport in Lagos is 0.750 (p-value 0.000

TABLE 1.2   Correlation matrix of Lagos Airport (LA), Airport in Lagos (AiL), and Lagos International Airport (LIA)

		LA	LIA	AiL
LA	Pearson Correlation	1		.602(**)
	Sig. (2-tailed)			.008
	N	18		18
LIA	Pearson Correlation	.724(**)	1	.750(**)
	Sig. (2-tailed)	.000		.000
	N	18	18	18
AiL	Pearson Correlation	.602(**)	.750(**)	1
	Sig. (2-tailed)	.008	.000	
	N	18	18	18

** Correlation is significant at the 0.01 level (2-tailed)

< 0.01), which revealed that there is a positive and significant relationship between the data of search terms of Lagos International Airport and Airport in Lagos. The above information implies that the search queries of Lagos Airport and Lagos International Airport are related, and the search queries of Lagos International Airport and Airport in Lagos are related. All the correlation values are close to 1, which indicates that air travelers tend to behave similarly while arranging a visit to Lagos; as a consequence, government agencies and other interested parties will be able to prepare for air travel-related activities in Lagos, and service all the necessary infrastructures in the MMIA.

1.4.2 Suitability of Google Trend Data for Forecasting

The total number of Google trends from 2004 to 2021, as well as the total number of actual passenger throughputs in MMIA within the same period was shown in Table 1.3. Correlation was employed to assess the forecasting adequacy. The nearer the correlation value is to 1, the better the data for forecasting. As revealed in Table 1.4, the correlation value between actual passenger throughputs in MMIA and Google Trend for passenger

TABLE 1.3   Total Google Trends and actual passenger throughputs in MMIA

Year	Sum of Google Trends	Actual
Yr 2004	1,192	1,943,601
Yr 2005	1,171	2,102,601
Yr 2006	1,067	2,152,315
Yr 2007	1,038	2,430,224
Yr 2008	1,052	2,688,595
Yr 2009	1,058	2,324,469
Yr 2010	1,086	2,409,087
Yr 2011	1,248	2,619,190
Yr 2012	1,232	3,232,462
Yr 2013	1,265	3,877,840
Yr 2014	1,287	2,582,288
Yr 2015	1,326	3,024,078
Yr 2016	1,415	2,945,914
Yr 2017	1,490	2,832,418
Yr 2018	1,586	3,017,977
Yr 2019	1,305	3,202,837
Yr 2020	1,219	997,760
Yr 2021	1,453	1,095,027

Source: Google Trends (2022); FAAN (2022); NBS (2022)

TABLE 1.4   Correlation of Google Trends and actual passenger throughputs in MMIA

		Google Trend of Air Travel Demand in Lagos
Actual Passenger Throughputs in MMIA	Pearson Correlation	.169
	Sig. (2-tailed)	.502

Source: Google Trends (2022)

throughputs in Lagos Airport is very low (0.169), implying that Google Trend data cannot be suitable for forecasting passenger throughputs in MMIA.

The presence of consistent and strong associations between the search terms does not imply that there would be a relationship between the Google trend data of aggregate search terms and the exact data, as demonstrated in this study. It means that just a small number of the search terms may be utilized to plan future airport demand in MMIA. The information search and visit, on the other hand, confirms that air travelers search for International Airport in Lagos immediately before or during a trip [41], enhancing the travel agencies, airlines, airport management, and other stakeholders to assess their immediate demand using online search data, but again the appropriate keywords must be found.

The Google search engine has 16.9% market share in the Lagos international air travel markets, which is less than 80%, making it unsuitable for Google to be regarded as the exclusive source of search query data. According to Artola *et al.* [42], the use of data gathered from search engines may result in underestimated or inflated estimates, posing a challenge to the selection of keywords [43]. According to Baker and Fradkin [44], the significant keywords should make known individual word linkages between a search query and an investigated phenomenon, while leaving out word combinations or single words that may be used to meet another information demand. This finding is consistent with the findings of [45].

1.5 CONCLUSION

The study examined the forecasting of airport passenger demand in Murtala Muhammed International Airport (MMIA) using Google Trends. It explored the dynamics of Google Trends such that the data provided by Google Trends are employed for forecasting air passenger throughputs in MMIA in Lagos. The relationship between the search terms for actual passenger throughputs (worldwide) for 18 years (2004–2021) was achieved using Google Trends. Google Trends is a source of data that is suitable for timely information. The study found that three variables: Lagos Airport (LA), Airport in Lagos (AiL), and Lagos International Airport (LIA) have higher searches, therefore they are suitable for predicting customer journeys to MMIA for air travel purposes.

The correlation between the search queries of Lagos Airport and Lagos International Airport is 0.724 (p-value 0.000 < 0.01) and between the search queries of Lagos International Airport and Airport in Lagos is 0.750 (p-value 0.000 < 0.01), which revealed a positive and significant relationship, which implies that the search queries of Lagos Airport and Lagos International Airport are related, and the search queries of Lagos International Airport and Airport in Lagos are related. The correlation between the total number of Google trends from 2004to 2021, as well as the total number of actual passenger throughputs in MMIA within the same period, is very low (0.169), implying that Google Trend data cannot be suitable for forecasting passenger throughputs in MMIA.

It is well recognized that Google Trends has grown to be one of the most extensively utilized free resources for forecasters in academia, the corporate sector, and both the public and private sectors. Numerous studies from numerous disciplines have come to the conclusion that Google Trends increases forecast accuracy. Even if the same search phrase, information, and location is used, each sample of Google search data is unique, despite this seemingly widespread ignorance. This implies that arbitrary conclusions can be discovered only by chance.

It is essential to note that popular phrases do not differ much amongst various samples. Our words of interest, however, are not often those that are so well-liked. Therefore, a more reliable time series of that term can be obtained by collecting a variety of samples and averaging them across each term. It is crucial to remember that if a sample appears on one average, it inevitably does not appear on the other.

REFERENCES

1. N. Woloszko, "Tracking activity in real time with Google Trends," OCDE, Dec. 2020. doi: 10.1787/6b9c7518-en.
2. O. Omisore, K. Eri, and S. O. Paul, "Federal Airports Authority of Nigeria (FAAN): A chronological description of its functionality in the aviation industry," *Journal of Good Governance and Sustainable Development in Africa*, vol. 2, no. 2, pp. 193–202, 2014.

3. A. Ao and S. Ms, "The dynamics for evaluating forecasting methods for international air passenger demand in Nigeria," *J Tourism Hospit*, vol. 7, no. 4, 2018, doi: 10.4172/2167-0269.1000366.

4. B. Thompson, "Airport retailing in the UK," *Journal of Retail & Leisure Property*, vol. 6, pp. 203–211, 2007.

5. S. Mitric, "Urban transport lending by the World Bank: The last decade," *Research in Transportation Economics*, vol. 40, no. 1, pp. 19–33, 2013.

6. Z. Xiang, D. Wang, J. T. O'Leary, and D. R. Fesenmaier, "Adapting to the internet: Trends in travelers' use of the web for trip planning," *Journal of Travel Research*, vol. 54, no. 4, pp. 511–527, 2015.

7. J. Mabrouki, M. Benbouzid, D. Dhiba, and S. El Hajjaji, "Internet of things for monitoring and detection of agricultural production," in *Intelligent Systems in Big Data, Semantic Web and Machine Learning*, Springer, pp. 271–282, 2021.

8. M. Mohy-eddine, A. Guezzaz, S. Benkirane, and M. Azrour, "IoT-enabled smart agriculture: Security issues and applications," in *Artificial Intelligence and Smart Environment: ICAISE'2022*, Springer, pp. 566–571, 2023.

9. S. Dargaoui *et al.*, "An overview of the security challenges in IoT environment," in *Advanced Technology for Smart Environment and Energy*, J. Mabrouki, A. Mourade, A. Irshad, and S. A. Chaudhry, Eds., in Environmental Science and Engineering. Springer International Publishing, 2023, pp. 151–160. doi: 10.1007/978-3-031-25662-2_13.

10. C. Hazman, S. Benkirane, A. Guezzaz, M. Azrour, and M. Abdedaime, "Intrusion detection framework for IoT-based smart environments security," in *Artificial Intelligence and Smart Environment: ICAISE'2022*, Springer, pp. 546–552, 2023.

11. M. Mohy-eddine, S. Benkirane, A. Guezzaz, and M. Azrour, "Random forest-based IDS for IIoT edge computing security using ensemble learning for dimensionality reduction." International Journal of Embedded Systems, vol. 15, no. 6, pp. 467–474, 2022.

12. G. Fattah, J. Mabrouki, F. Ghrissi, M. Azrour, and Y. Abrouki, "Multi-sensor system and Internet of Things (IoT) technologies for air pollution monitoring," in *Futuristic Research Trends and Applications of Internet of Things*, Bhawana Rudra, Anshul Verma, Shekhar Verma, Bhanu Shrestha, Eds., CRC Press, 2022, pp. 101–116.

13. J. Mabrouki, M. Azrour, and S. E. Hajjaji, "Use of internet of things for monitoring and evaluating water's quality: A comparative study," *International Journal of Cloud Computing*, vol. 10, no. 5–6, pp. 633–644, 2021.

14. M. Douiba, S. Benkirane, A. Guezzaz, and M. Azrour, "An improved anomaly detection model for IoT security using decision tree and gradient boosting," *The Journal of Supercomputing*, vol. 79, no. 3 , pp. 1–20, 2022.

15. S. Amaouche *et al.*, "FSCB-IDS: Feature selection and minority class balancing for attacks detection in VANETS," *Applied sciences*, 2023.

16. M. Benzyane, I. Zeroual, M. Azrour, and S. Agoujil, "Convolutional long short-term memory network model for dynamic texture classification: A case study," in *International Conference on Advanced Intelligent Systems for*

Sustainable Development, J. Kacprzyk, M. Ezziyyani, and V. E. Balas, Eds., in Lecture Notes in Networks and Systems. Springer Nature Switzerland, pp. 383–395, 2023. doi: 10.1007/978-3-031-26384-2_33.

17. S. Khan *et al.*, "Manufacturing industry based on dynamic soft sensors in integrated with feature representation and classification using fuzzy logic and deep learning architecture," *Int J Adv Manuf Technol*, Jun. 2023, doi: 10.1007/s00170-023-11602-y.

18. M. K. Boutahir, Y. Farhaoui, and M. Azrour, "Machine learning and deep learning applications for solar radiation predictions review: Morocco as a case of study," in *Digital Economy, Business Analytics, and Big Data Analytics Applications*, Saad G. Yaseen, Ed., Springer, pp. 55–67, 2022.

19. A. Guezzaz, A. Asimi, A. Mourade, Z. Tbatou, and Y. Asimi, "A multi-layer perceptron classifier for monitoring network traffic," in *Big Data and Networks Technologies 3*, Yousef Farhaoui Ed., Springer, pp. 262–270, 2020.

20. M. Mohy-Eddine, M. Azrour, J. Mabrouki, F. Amounas, A. Guezzaz, and S. Benkirane, "Embedded web server implementation for real-time water monitoring," in *Advanced Technology for Smart Environment and Energy*, J. Mabrouki, A. Mourade, A. Irshad, and S. A. Chaudhry, Eds., in Environmental Science and Engineering. Springer International Publishing, pp. 301–311, 2023. doi: 10.1007/978-3-031-25662-2_24.

21. J. Mabrouki, M. Azrour, A. Boubekraoui, and S. El Hajjaji, "Intelligent system for the protection of people," in *Intelligent Systems in Big Data, Semantic Web and Machine Learning*, Noreddine Gherabi and Janusz Kacprzyk, Eds., Springer, pp. 157–165, 2021.

22. M. Mohy-eddine, A. Guezzaz, S. Benkirane, and M. Azrour, "An effective intrusion detection approach based on ensemble learning for IIoT edge computing," *Journal of Computer Virology and Hacking Techniques*, pp. 1–13, 2022. https://doi.org/10.1007/s11416-022-00456-9

23. M. Douiba, S. Benkirane, A. Guezzaz, and M. Azrour, "Anomaly detection model based on gradient boosting and decision tree for IoT environments security," *Journal of Reliable Intelligent Environments*, pp. 1–12, 2022. https://doi.org/10.1007/s40860-022-00184-3

24. J. Mabrouki, G. Fattah, S. Kherraf, Y. Abrouki, M. Azrour, and S. El Hajjaji, "Artificial intelligence system for intelligent monitoring and management of water treatment plants," in *Emerging Real-World Applications of Internet of Things*, Anshul Verma, Pradeepika Verma, Yousef Farhaoui, Zhihan Lv, Eds., CRC Press, pp. 69–87, 2022.

25. M. Azrour, Y. Farhaoui, M. Ouanan, and A. Guezzaz, "SPIT detection in telephony over IP using K-means algorithm," *Procedia Computer Science*, vol. 148, pp. 542–551, 2019, doi: 10.1016/j.procs.2019.01.027.

26. U. S. Peceny, J. Urbančič, S. Mokorel, V. Kuralt, and T. Ilijaš, "Tourism 4.0: Challenges in marketing a paradigm shift," in *Consumer Behavior and Marketing*, Matthew Reyes, Ed., IntechOpen, 2019, pp. 39–58.

27. M. Balasaraswathi, K. Srinivasan, L. Udayakumar, S. Sivasakthiselvan, and M. G. Sumithra, "Big data analytic of contexts and cascading tourism for smart city," *Materials Today: Proceedings*, 2020.

28. H. Song, G. Li, S. F. Witt, and B. Fei, "Tourism demand modelling and forecasting: How should demand be measured?" *Tourism Economics*, vol. 16, no. 1, pp. 63–81, 2010.

29. J. Kumar and K. Hussain, "Evaluating tourism's economic effects: Comparison of different approaches," *Procedia-Social and Behavioral Sciences*, vol. 144, pp. 360–365, 2014.

30. K. S. Pradeep and K. Rajesh, "IJETT - The evaluation of forecasting methods for sales of sterilized flavoured milk in Chhattisgarh," *International Journal of Engineering Trends and Technology - IJETT*, vol. 8, no. 2, pp. 98–104, 2014.

31. G. Bernard and P. Andritsos, "A process mining based model for customer journey mapping," in *Forum and Doctoral Consortium Papers Presented at the 29th International Conference on Advanced Information Systems Engineering (CAiSE 2017)*, CEUR Workshop Proceedings, 2017, pp. 49–56.

32. H. Choi and H. Varian, "Predicting the present with Google trends," *Economic Record*, vol. 88, no. s1, pp. 2–9, 2012, doi: 10.1111/j.1475-4932.2012.00809.x.

33. S. Seabold and A. Coppola, "Nowcasting prices using Google trends: An application to Central America," *World Bank Policy Research Working Paper*, no. 7398, 2015.

34. H. Song and H. Liu, "Predicting tourist demand using big data," in *Analytics in Smart Tourism Design: Concepts and Methods*, Zheng Xiang and Daniel R. Fesenmaier, Eds., 2017, pp. 13–29.

35. K. Lehman, M. Wickham, and D. Reiser, "Modelling the government/cultural tourism marketing interface," *Tourism Planning & Development*, vol. 14, no. 4, pp. 467–482, 2017.

36. S. Doerr and L. Gambacorta, "Identifying regions at risk with Google trends: The impact of Covid-19 on US labour markets," Apr. 2020, Accessed: Jun. 14, 2023. [Online]. Available: https://www.bis.org/publ/bisbull08.htm

37. L. Ferrara and A. Simoni, "When are Google data useful to nowcast GDP? An approach via preselection and shrinkage," *Journal of Business & Economic Statistics*, pp. 1–15, 2022.

38. F. Li and P. S. Yip, "How to make adjustments of underreporting of suicide by place, gender, and age in China?" *Social psychiatry and Psychiatric Epidemiology*, vol. 55, pp. 1133–1143, 2020.

39. B. Lobe, D. Morgan, and K. A. Hoffman, "Qualitative data collection in an era of social distancing," *International Journal of Qualitative Methods*, vol. 19, p. 1609406920937875, 2020.

40. H. Song and G. Li, "Tourism demand modelling and forecasting—A review of recent research," *Tourism Management*, vol. 29, no. 2, pp. 203–220, 2008.

41. Z. Xiang and B. Pan, "Travel queries on cities in the United States: Implications for search engine marketing for tourist destinations," *Tourism Management*, vol. 32, no. 1, pp. 88–97, 2011.

42. C. Artola and E. Martínez-Galán, "Tracking the future on the web: Construction of leading indicators using internet searches," *Banco de Espana Occasional Paper*, no. 1203, 2012.

43. F. D'Amuri and J. Marcucci, "The predictive power of Google searches in forecasting US unemployment," *International Journal of Forecasting*, vol. 33, no. 4, pp. 801–816, 2017.
44. S. R. Baker and A. Fradkin, "The impact of unemployment insurance on job search: Evidence from Google search data," *Review of Economics and Statistics*, vol. 99, no. 5, pp. 756–768, 2017.
45. A. Naccarato, S. Falorsi, S. Loriga, and A. Pierini, "Combining official and Google trends data to forecast the Italian youth unemployment rate," *Technological Forecasting and Social Change*, vol. 130, pp. 114–122, 2018.

CHAPTER 2

Blockchain Technology Overview: Architecture, Proposed and Future Trends

Divya Prakash, Shaik Yasmin, M. Preethi, Ghufran Ahmad Khan, Taushif Anwar, and G. Krishna Mohan

2.1 INTRODUCTION

Blockchain is a type of distributed ledger technology that allows for the secure and transparent recording of transactions among multiple parties within a decentralized network. Its architecture consists of three main components: a network of nodes, a consensus algorithm, and a data structure. The decentralized network of computers, or nodes, collectively maintains the blockchain database. Each node has a copy of the blockchain and can participate in the validation and verification of transactions. The consensus mechanism is a set of rules that govern how transactions are validated and incorporated into the blockchain. These techniques ensure that all nodes on the network agree on the current state of the blockchain and prevent malicious actors from altering its history. BT utilizes a sequential

DOI: 10.1201/9781003438779-2

chain of blocks to store transaction data, with each block containing a cryptographic hash of the previous block. This approach guarantees the integrity and immutability of the blockchain and extends beyond financial transactions to other fields such as the Internet of Things (IoT) [1–13]. By using blockchain, IoT devices can securely exchange data while maintaining data integrity. Future developments in BT include merging it with other emerging technologies like artificial intelligence (AI), machine learning (ML), and the Internet of Things (IoT)

This integration can provide new use cases for BT and increase its adoption [14]. Future trends in BT include the development of new consensus mechanisms that are more energy-efficient and the adoption of BT by governments and institutions for secure data sharing and management. Additionally, BT may play a crucial role in the development of decentralized finance (DeFi) and the tokenization of assets [15]. In 1991, Stuart Haber and W. Scott Stornetta introduced the concept of BT with the aim of making digital documents timestamped and tamper-proof. Although their work laid the foundation for BT, it was not until the advent of Bitcoin in 2008 that blockchain was significantly implemented. Since then, BT has advanced and found widespread use in diverse industries, such as finance, healthcare, and supply chain management (Figure 2.1).

BT is being widely employed to build safe, decentralized, and impenetrable data management and storage systems. Multiple parties can access the same data and must concur on any changes to the system because it runs on a distributed ledger [16]. BT has enormous potential applications, and in the years ahead, we'll probably continue to see new, creative applications for it. In 2004, Hal Finney, who was both a computer scientist and a crypto activist, designed an A-system for a reusable digital currency. He developed a prototype form of cryptocurrency called Proof-of-Work (RPoW), which was a crucial milestone in the advancement of digital currencies. The RPoW mechanism produces an RSA-signed token that people can exchange with each other in exchange for non-flooding Hash cash-based Proof-of-Work tokens. RPoW ensures that double-spending is avoided by creating a record of token ownership on a dependable server. People from any location can promptly confirm the accuracy and entirety of the data on this server.

The concept of distributed blockchains was developed by Satoshi Nakamoto in 2008 [17]. The modification of adding blocks to the initial chain without needing verification from a third party greatly enhanced the design. This new tree structure securely documents the transfer of

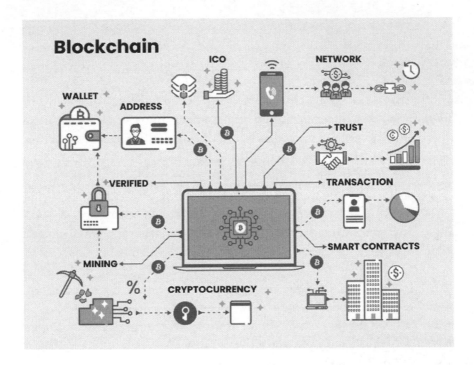

FIGURE 2.1   Usage of blockchain

data and utilizes a peer-to-peer network to validate and timestamp every transaction. It operates independently without the need for centralized authority. These improvements have made blockchains the basis of cryptocurrencies, and this design is now utilized to manage a public ledger of all Bitcoin transactions. The advancement of the blockchain has been steady and encouraging. In Satoshi Nakamoto's original paper, the phrases "block" and "chain" were used separately; nevertheless, it wasn't until 2016 that the term "blockchain" gained popularity. A blockchain for a cryptocurrency, which keeps track of all transactions on the network, recently went from 20 GB to 100 GB in size [18].

2.2 EVOLUTION OF BLOCKCHAIN

Since its beginnings, BT has gone through various stages of evolution. An overview of the many stages of blockchain advancement is provided below:

- Genesis phase: The first blockchain, Bitcoin, was created in 2009, marking the beginning of the Genesis phase. Initially developed as a decentralized digital currency, Bitcoin aimed to facilitate peer-to-peer transactions without intermediaries such as banks. The introduction of multiple cryptocurrencies based on Bitcoin's BT signaled the start of the Genesis phase [19].

- Altcoin phase: The Altcoin phase began with the introduction of alternative cryptocurrencies like Litecoin, Namecoin, and Ripple that were distinct from Bitcoin. This phase brought new capabilities to BT such as support for smart contracts, diverse consensus techniques, and faster transaction times [15].

- Enterprise phase: In 2015, major corporations like IBM, Microsoft, and JP Morgan began exploring the potential of BT [19], marking the start of the Enterprise phase. These corporations recognized the potential of blockchain to streamline their operations and reduce costs, leading to the creation of private or permissioned blockchains accessible only to specific users.

- Initial Coin Offering (ICO) phase: In 2017, blockchain firms started to raise money by issuing their own cryptocurrencies or tokens, which is when the ICO phase started. These tokens were primarily used to access blockchain-based services or as a form of payment within the blockchain ecosystem [20].

- Decentralized Finance (DeFi) phase: In 2019, BT was first applied to develop decentralized financial applications such as lending and borrowing platforms, decentralized exchanges, and stablecoins. This was the beginning of the DeFi phase. Users were able to access financial services through these DeFi applications without the aid of middlemen like banks or brokers.

- Non-Fungible Token (NFT) phase: In 2021, the NFT phase began, in which special digital assets that could be purchased, sold, and exchanged were created using BT. With several high-profile sales of NFT-based artworks, NFTs garnered a lot of interest in the art world. All things considered, BT has developed from a straightforward peer-to-peer payment system to a flexible platform that can be utilized for a range of applications (Figure 2.2).

FIGURE 2.2   Evaluation of blockchain

2.3 BLOCKCHAIN ARCHITECTURE

A blockchain system's architecture refers to its layout and construction. A blockchain is a type of ledger that is decentralized and distributed, allowing for secure, transparent, and immutable transactions. A blockchain system's architecture often comprises numerous levels, each with a distinct function and goal [21].

- Network layer: This layer includes the nodes that make up the blockchain network. Every individual node possesses a duplicate of the complete blockchain ledger and is capable of authenticating and confirming transactions.

- Consensus layer: This layer is responsible for reaching a consensus on the validity of transactions. Various consensus algorithms, such as Proof-of-Work and Proof-of-Stake, can be employed to accomplish this goal.

- Data layer: The actual data that is kept on the blockchain is contained in this layer. Every block of the blockchain holds a set of transactions, and once a block becomes a part of the chain, it is impossible to eliminate it.

- Smart contract layer: This layer enables the implementation of self-executing blockchain-based contracts. The automatic execution of smart contracts is preprogrammed to happen when specific criteria are satisfied.

- Application layer: This layer includes the user-facing applications that interact with the blockchain, such as wallets, exchanges, and other Apps (decentralized applications).

2.4 PROPOSED BLOCKCHAIN SOLUTIONS FOR SCALABILITY

By offering a safe, decentralized, and transparent network, BT has demonstrated enormous potential for revolutionizing numerous industries. Scalability, however, is one of the main problems that blockchain is now facing. Blockchain networks are now unable to keep up with the number of transactions, which causes longer processing times and higher transaction costs. Here are several blockchain scaling methods that have been suggested:

- Sharding: Sharding is the process of dividing the blockchain network into smaller segments known as shards. The capacity of the network is increased since each shard can handle transactions concurrently and independently [22]. This can greatly increase the blockchain's throughput and enable it to process a greater number of transactions.

- Scaling off-chain solutions: Off-chain scaling techniques entail transferring some transactions to auxiliary networks in addition to the primary blockchain network. These auxiliary networks can process a huge number of transactions and can later be reconciled with the primary blockchain network. The Lightning Network and Plasma are two examples of well-liked off-chain scaling techniques.

- Sidechains: Connected to the primary blockchain network, sidechains are autonomous blockchain networks. They have a high transaction volume capacity and can be used to move assets from one blockchain to another [23]. By lightening the burden on the network, they can increase the scalability of the primary blockchain network.

- Mechanisms of consensus: Blockchain networks require consensus methods, which have a big impact on scalability [24]. The scalability of blockchain networks can be considerably increased by lowering the cost of some suggested consensus techniques, such as Proof-of-Stake (PoS) and Delegated Proof-of-Stake (DPoS).

2.5 FUTURE TRENDS IN BT

The impact of BT on several industries such as finance, supply chain management, healthcare, and real estate has been notable. As the technology progresses further, there is a likelihood of witnessing interesting new developments and trends in the blockchain industry. Here are some potential future trends in BT:

- The growing acceptance of Decentralized Finance (DeFi) pertains to the implementation of BT in developing financial systems that function without intermediaries in a decentralized manner. DeFi platforms are built on blockchain networks and use smart contracts to automate financial transactions. As individuals become increasingly aware of the advantages of utilizing decentralized financial systems, it is likely that DeFi platforms will continue to expand in the future [25].

- The combination of BT and artificial intelligence (AI) has the potential to be highly impactful. Both technologies are known to be revolutionary, and their integration can result in the development of secure and efficient systems that can simplify complicated procedures. For example, blockchain-based AI systems can be used to verify the authenticity of data, prevent fraud, and enhance the security of financial transactions [26].

- As BT continues to mature, there will be a greater focus on privacy and security. One potential future trend is the development of blockchain-based systems that provide greater privacy and security for users. For example, we may see the development of privacy-focused blockchain networks that use advanced cryptography to protect user data [27].

- There is the potential for increased interoperability between blockchain networks. Currently, there are many different blockchain networks that operate independently of each other. However, in the future, we may witness enhanced compatibility among these networks, facilitating effortless exchange of assets and information across various blockchain networks. This will simplify the process of developing intricate systems that cover multiple networks [28].

- As more industries become aware of the potential benefits of BT, we can expect to see greater adoption of the technology in traditional industries such as banking, insurance, and healthcare. This could lead to the creation of new business models and the transformation of existing ones [29].

- Overall, the future of BT is very promising, and we can expect to see many exciting new developments in the years to come.

2.6 BLOCKCHAIN GOVERNANCE MODELS

Blockchain governance refers to the processes and structures used to make decisions about the operation and evolution of a blockchain network. There are several different governance models that have been proposed and implemented in various blockchain projects [30]. Here are some of the most common ones:

- Decentralized governance: In this model, decisions about the network are made through a decentralized voting process. Every participant in the network has a say in decision-making, and there is no central authority that controls the process. Examples of this model include Dash and EOS.

- Representative governance: In this model, participants elect representatives to make decisions on their behalf. The representatives are typically chosen based on their stake in the network, and they are responsible for making decisions that are in the best interest of their constituents. Examples of this model include Bit Shares and Risk.

- Foundation governance: In this model, a foundation is established to oversee the development and operation of the network. The foundation is typically governed by a board of directors, and its decisions are made based on the best interests of the network. Examples of this model include Ethereum and Ripple.

- Hybrid governance: This model combines elements of decentralized, representative, and foundation governance. It allows for a flexible and adaptable governance structure that can change over time as the needs of the network evolve. Examples of this model include Tezos and Polkadot.

It is worth noting that each governance model has its own advantages and disadvantages, and the choice of governance model largely depends on the specific needs and goals of the blockchain network.

2.7 THE SOCIAL AND ETHICAL IMPLICATIONS OF BLOCKCHAIN

BT has significant social and ethical implications that need to be considered as it becomes more widely adopted. These are some of the main causes for worry:

- Employment: BT has the potential to automate many processes that are currently performed by humans, which could lead to job losses in certain industries. However, it could also create new job opportunities in areas such as blockchain development, maintenance, and management [31].

- Privacy: Although BT is often touted for its security and privacy features, it can still pose privacy risks. For example, blockchain transactions are often publicly visible, which could lead to the identification of individuals or the exposure of sensitive information [32].

- Inequality: BT has the potential to create more equitable systems by reducing the need for intermediaries and increasing transparency. However, it could also exacerbate existing inequalities if access to technology is limited or if certain groups are disproportionately affected by its use [33].

- Environmental sustainability: The energy consumption of some blockchain networks, such as Bitcoin, has raised concerns about their environmental impact. The mining process used to create new blocks on these networks requires significant amounts of energy, which contributes to carbon emissions.

- Governance: The decentralized nature of BT raises questions about governance and accountability. Without a central authority, it can be difficult to make decisions or enforce rules. Additionally, the potential for manipulation or collusion by a small group of participants could undermine the integrity of the system [33].

In general, although BT could bring about significant changes in various societal areas, it is crucial to cautiously examine its ethical and social consequences and take necessary measures to mitigate any possible risks or adverse effects.

2.8 BLOCKCHAIN REGULATIONS AND LEGAL FRAMEWORKS

BT is still relatively new, and many countries are still working to establish legal frameworks and regulations to govern its use. However, there are some general trends that can be observed across various jurisdictions [34].

In general, BT is subject to the same laws and regulations that apply to other forms of technology, such as data protection, intellectual property, and contract law. However, BT also presents unique challenges and opportunities, particularly in the areas of security, privacy, and accountability.

- One of the key regulatory issues with BT is the question of how to classify and regulate different types of tokens, such as cryptocurrencies and utility tokens. Different countries have taken different approaches to this issue, with some countries treating certain types of tokens as securities, while others have opted for a more flexible approach [32].

- Another important issue is the regulation of blockchain-based businesses and services, such as cryptocurrency exchanges and Initial Coin Offerings (ICOs). Many countries have introduced licensing and registration requirements for these businesses, as well as guidelines on best practices for security and transparency.

- The regulations governing BT are continually changing, and it is crucial for individuals and companies involved in this field to remain informed about the most recent legal advancements in their respective regions.

2.9 BLOCKCHAIN'S EFFECTS ON SOCIETY AND ETHICS

BT has the potential to revolutionize many aspects of society, but it also presents several social and ethical implications that must be carefully considered.

- One of the key social implications of BT is its potential to disrupt traditional power structures. Blockchain allows for decentralized systems and peer-to-peer transactions, which can challenge the authority of centralized institutions such as banks, governments, and other intermediaries [35]. This can have both positive and negative effects, depending on the specific use case and the broader social and political context.

- Another social implication of BT is its potential impact on privacy and data protection. While BT is designed to be highly secure and transparent, the immutable nature of the blockchain means that once data is recorded, it cannot be deleted or modified. This raises concerns about the potential for sensitive personal data to be stored on the blockchain and accessed without an individual's consent or control.

- Ethically, the use of BT also raises questions about accountability and responsibility. Because blockchain systems are often decentralized and trustless, it can be difficult to attribute responsibility for actions taken on the blockchain or to hold individuals or organizations accountable for their actions. This can create a sense of moral hazard and undermine traditional systems of justice and accountability [32].

Finally, the social and ethical implications of BT also include issues around economic inequality, access to technology, and the potential for exploitation and abuse. As with any new technology, it is important to consider the potential social and ethical implications of BT and to work proactively to mitigate any negative effects.

2.10 BLOCKCHAIN USE CASES IN VARIOUS INDUSTRIES

By offering a safe and transparent platform for data storage and sharing, BT has the potential to revolutionize a number of industries [33]. Here are a few examples of BT's applications across various industries:

- Finance: The financial sector is where BT is most used. Cross-border payments can be made more quickly and inexpensively by using BT to provide a safe and open system for transactions. In order to lower the possibility of fraud and increase transparency, it can also be used to construct a tamper-proof ledger of transactions.

- Supply chain: A decentralized system for tracking products along the supply chain can be made using BT [36]. Businesses may track products in real-time using BT to make sure they are delivered to the correct customers.

- Real estate: A secure and open system for property transactions can be established using BT. Buyers and sellers may track the ownership of properties and ensure that all transactions are carried out properly by using BT. This can lower the possibility of fraud and increase the effectiveness of real estate deals.

- Education: A decentralized system for evaluating academic credentials can be developed using BT. Educational institutions can build safe and unchangeable records of students' accomplishments by utilizing BT [37]. This can increase the effectiveness of the hiring process and lower the possibility of credential forgery.

- Energy: A decentralized system for tracking energy generation and consumption can be developed using BT. Energy providers can monitor production using BT.

2.11 CONCLUSION

BT has evolved significantly since its inception, and it has the potential to revolutionize various industries. Its distributed and decentralized nature provides greater transparency and security in transactions, making it a viable solution for businesses and individuals. The architecture of BT, including its consensus mechanisms and smart contract capabilities, allows the creation of innovative applications and services. However, as with any technology, there are also social and ethical implications to consider. The decentralization of power and authority may challenge traditional models of governance, and the anonymity of transactions may create opportunities for illicit activities. Looking toward the future, BT is expected to continue to grow and mature with the emergence of new use cases and applications. The adoption of BT by governments and large corporations may accelerate its mainstream acceptance. However, there are also challenges to overcome, such as scalability and interoperability issues.

REFERENCES

1. M. Azrour, M. Ouanan, Y. Farhaoui, and A. Guezzaz, "Security analysis of Ye et al. authentication protocol for Internet of Things," in *Big Data and Smart Digital Environment*, Springer, 2019, pp. 67–74.
2. S. Amaouche *et al.*, "FSCB-IDS: Feature selection and minority class balancing for attacks detection in VANETS," *Applied Sciences*, vol. 13, no. 13, p. 7488, 2023.
3. M. K. Boutahir, Y. Farhaoui, and M. Azrour, "Machine learning and deep learning applications for solar radiation predictions review: Morocco as a case of study," in *Digital Economy, Business Analytics, and Big Data Analytics Applications*, Springer, 2022, pp. 55–67.

4. J. Mabrouki, M. Benbouzid, D. Dhiba, and S. El Hajjaji, "Internet of Things for monitoring and detection of agricultural production," in *Intelligent Systems in Big Data, Semantic Web and Machine Learning*, Springer, 2021, pp. 271–282.

5. M. Mohy-eddine, A. Guezzaz, S. Benkirane, and M. Azrour, "IoT-enabled smart agriculture: Security issues and applications," in *Artificial Intelligence and Smart Environment: ICAISE'2022*, Springer, 2023, pp. 566–571.

6. S. Dargaoui *et al.*, "An overview of the security challenges in IoT environment," in *Advanced Technology for Smart Environment and Energy*, J. Mabrouki, A. Mourade, A. Irshad, and S. A. Chaudhry, Eds., in Environmental Science and Engineering. Springer International Publishing, 2023, pp. 151–160. doi: 10.1007/978-3-031-25662-2_13.

7. M. Mohy-Eddine, M. Azrour, J. Mabrouki, F. Amounas, A. Guezzaz, and S. Benkirane, "Embedded web server implementation for real-time water monitoring," in *Advanced Technology for Smart Environment and Energy*, J. Mabrouki, A. Mourade, A. Irshad, and S. A. Chaudhry, Eds., in Environmental Science and Engineering. Springer International Publishing, 2023, pp. 301–311. doi: 10.1007/978-3-031-25662-2_24.

8. C. Hazman, S. Benkirane, A. Guezzaz, M. Azrour, and M. Abdedaime, "Intrusion detection framework for IoT-based smart environments security," in *Artificial Intelligence and Smart Environment: ICAISE'2022*, Springer, 2023, pp. 546–552.

9. H. Attou, A. Guezzaz, S. Benkirane, M. Azrour, and Y. Farhaoui, "Cloud-based intrusion detection approach using machine learning techniques," *Big Data Mining and Analytics*, vol. 6, no. 3, pp. 311–320, 2023.

10. M. Mohy-eddine, S. Benkirane, A. Guezzaz, and M. Azrour, "Random forest-based IDS for IIoT edge computing security using ensemble learning for dimensionality reduction." vol. 15, no. 6, pp. 467–474, 2023.

11. M. Mohy-eddine, A. Guezzaz, S. Benkirane, and M. Azrour, "An efficient network intrusion detection model for IoT security using K-NN classifier and feature selection," *Multimedia Tools and Applications*, 2023, doi: 10.1007/s11042-023-14795-2.

12. M. Douiba, S. Benkirane, A. Guezzaz, and M. Azrour, "An improved anomaly detection model for IoT security using decision tree and gradient boosting," *The Journal of Supercomputing*, vol. 79, no. 3, pp. 3392–3411, 2023.

13. M. Douiba, S. Benkirane, A. Guezzaz, and M. Azrour, "Anomaly detection model based on gradient boosting and decision tree for IoT environments security," *Journal of Reliable Intelligent Environments*, pp. 1–12, 2022. https://doi.org/10.1007/s40860-022-00184-3

14. M. M. Queiroz, R. Telles, and S. H. Bonilla, "Blockchain and supply chain management integration: A systematic review of the literature," *Supply Chain Management: An International Journal*, vol. 25, no. 2, pp. 241–254, 2020.

15. M. Swan, *Blockchain: Blueprint for a new economy*. O'Reilly Media, Inc., 2015.

16. S. Haber and W. S. Stornetta, *How to time-stamp a digital document.* Springer, 1991.
17. S. Nakamoto and A. Bitcoin, "A peer-to-peer electronic cash system," *Bitcoin–URL: https://bitcoin. org/bitcoin. pdf,* vol. 4, no. 2, p. 15, 2008.
18. M. Jakobsson and A. Juels, "Proofs of work and bread pudding protocols," in *Secure Information Networks: Communications and Multimedia Security IFIP TC6/TC11 Joint Working Conference on Communications and Multimedia Security (CMS'99) September 20–21, 1999, Leuven, Belgium,* Springer, 1999, pp. 258–272.
19. N. Radziwill, "Blockchain revolution: How the technology behind Bitcoin is changing money, business, and the world," *The Quality Management Journal,* vol. 25, no. 1, pp. 64–65, 2018.
20. S. Pahlajani, A. Kshirsagar, and V. Pachghare, "Survey on private blockchain consensus algorithms," in *2019 1st International Conference on Innovations in Information and Communication Technology (ICIICT),* IEEE, 2019, pp. 1–6.
21. L.-H. Zhu, B.-K. Zheng, M. Shen, F. Gao, H.-Y. Li, and K.-X. Shi, "Data security and privacy in bitcoin system: A survey," *Journal of Computer Science and Technology,* vol. 35, pp. 843–862, 2020.
22. D. Yang, C. Long, H. Xu, and S. Peng, "A review on scalability of blockchain," in *Proceedings of the 2020 the 2nd International Conference on Blockchain Technology,* 2020, pp. 1–6.
23. J. Poon and T. Dryja, "The bitcoin lightning network: Scalable off-chain instant payments," 2016.
24. C. Mao, A.-D. Nguyen, and W. Golab, "Performance and fault tolerance trade-offs in sharded permissioned blockchains," in *2021 3rd Conference on Blockchain Research & Applications for Innovative Networks and Services (BRAINS),* IEEE, 2021, pp. 185–192.
25. F. Schär, "Decentralized finance: On blockchain-and smart contract-based financial markets," *FRB of St. Louis Review,* 2021.
26. S. Mithas, Z.-L. Chen, T. J. Saldanha, and A. De Oliveira Silveira, "How will artificial intelligence and Industry 4.0 emerging technologies transform operations management?," *Production and Operations Management,* vol. 31, no. 12, pp. 4475–4487, 2022.
27. X. Li, P. Jiang, T. Chen, X. Luo, and Q. Wen, "A survey on the security of blockchain systems," *Future Generation Computer Systems,* vol. 107, pp. 841–853, 2020.
28. G. Wang, Q. Wang, and S. Chen, "Exploring blockchains interoperability: A systematic survey," *ACM Computing Surveys,* vol. 55, no. 13s, pp. 1–38, 2023.
29. C. Meske, I. Amojo, A.-S. Poncette, and F. Balzer, "The potential role of digital nudging in the digital transformation of the healthcare industry," in *Design, User Experience, and Usability. Application Domains: 8th International Conference, DUXU 2019, Held as Part of the 21st HCI International Conference, HCII 2019, Orlando, FL, USA, July 26–31, 2019, Proceedings, Part III 21,* Springer, 2019, pp. 323–336.

30. Y. Liu, Q. Lu, G. Yu, H.-Y. Paik, and L. Zhu, "Defining blockchain governance principles: A comprehensive framework," *Information Systems*, vol. 109, p. 102090, 2022.

31. W. Yang, S. Garg, A. Raza, D. Herbert, and B. Kang, "Blockchain: Trends and future," in *Knowledge Management and Acquisition for Intelligent Systems: 15th Pacific Rim Knowledge Acquisition Workshop, PKAW 2018, Nanjing, China, August 28–29, 2018, Proceedings 15*, Springer, 2018, pp. 201–210.

32. N. Kshetri, "1 Blockchain's roles in meeting key supply chain management objectives," *International Journal of Information Management*, vol. 39, pp. 80–89, 2018.

33. I. Pitas and A. N. Venetsanopoulos, *Nonlinear digital filters: Principles and applications*, vol. 84. Springer Science & Business Media, 2013.

34. H. Halaburda and M. Sarvary, *Beyond bitcoin*. Springer, 2022.

35. M. Alazab, S. Alhyari, A. Awajan, and A. B. Abdallah, "Blockchain technology in supply chain management: An empirical study of the factors affecting user adoption/acceptance," *Cluster Computing*, vol. 24, pp. 83–101, 2021.

36. M. Zhou, R. Liang, Z. Zhou, and X. Dong, "Combining high energy efficiency and fast charge-discharge capability in novel BaTiO3-based relaxor ferroelectric ceramic for energy-storage," *Ceramics International*, vol. 45, no. 3, pp. 3582–3590, 2019.

37. A. Wright and P. De Filippi, *Blockchain and the law: The rule of code*. Harvard University Press, 2018.

CHAPTER 3

Innovative Approach for Optimized IoT Security Based on Spatial Network Voronoï Diagrams, Network Centrality, and ML-enabled Blockchain

Aziz Mabrouk

3.1 INTRODUCTION

Due to the rapid expansion of the Internet of Things (IoT), ensuring the security of IoT networks has become a crucial concern. The consequences of an attack on these networks can be extremely devastating, particularly as it poses a threat to the confidentiality, integrity, and availability of data. Furthermore, the decentralized and highly interconnected nature of IoT networks makes them particularly vulnerable to attacks.

DOI: 10.1201/9781003438779-3

Various approaches have been suggested to bolster the security of IoT networks, including default security, network management, behavioral analysis, cryptography, and machine learning. However, these solutions have their own constraints and may prove inadequate in the face of rapidly evolving and increasingly complex IoT security threats.

In this paper, we present a novel approach to enhance the security of IoT networks by combining spatial network Voronoï diagrams, network centrality, and machine learning-enabled blockchain. We will provide an in-depth explanation of the foundations and principles of our method, as well as its key elements and their interactions. We will also describe the techniques and methodologies that we employ to identify critical IoT devices, prioritize security actions, design resilient networks, and detect and prevent attacks. We will then compare our method to current IoT security techniques and examine its potential applications across various sectors. Lastly, we will examine the advantages and implications of our method for researchers, practitioners, and decision-makers, and propose future research directions and areas for experimentation.

3.2 EXISTING APPROACHES FOR IOT SECURITY

3.2.1 Default Secure Approach

The default secure approach for IoT devices is a proactive strategy aiming to integrate security from the conception and manufacturing of the devices, as outlined by Adat and Gupta (2018) and Al-Fuqaha and Guizani (2015). This approach relies on the inclusion of robust security features in the hardware and software of IoT devices, the use of secure communication protocols, and the implementation of strong authentication and encryption measures.

The research of Alaba et al. (2017) corroborates the importance of this approach, emphasizing the adoption of security by design principles, which can help reduce potential vulnerabilities in IoT. They also highlight that default security can not only prevent a wide variety of security vulnerabilities but also offer increased resilience to attacks.

However, despite these advantages, it is important to note that implementing these security measures can be costly, posing a particular challenge for small IoT device manufacturers. Furthermore, while default security can help prevent many vulnerabilities, it cannot protect against all forms of threats, including those that exploit human errors or unknown vulnerabilities. Alaba et al. point out that default security cannot prevent all types of threats, particularly those that exploit human errors and software vulnerabilities. Therefore, a multi-layered security approach that also includes mechanisms for detecting and responding to incidents is required.

3.2.2 Network Management-Based Approach

The network management-based approach for IoT security involves monitoring and controlling network activities using tools such as intrusion detection systems, firewalls, and identity management systems (Zarpelão, Miani, Kawakani, & de Alvarenga, 2017). This approach can allow real-time detection and prevention of attacks, an important aspect of IoT network security (Kolias, Kambourakis, Stavrou, & Voas, 2017).

However, implementing this approach can be complex and costly, particularly for large IoT networks (Alrawais, Alhothaily, Hu, & Cheng, 2017). Moreover, it may not be fully effective against sophisticated attacks that use advanced evasion techniques (Frustaci, Pace, Aloi, & Fortino, 2018).

It's also important to note that network management for IoT systems could benefit from the integration of emerging technologies like blockchain for safer and more efficient network management. Despite the challenges, this approach is important to addressing security challenges to the Internet of Things (Sfar, Natalizio, Challal, & Chtourou, 2018).

3.2.3 Behavioral Analysis-Based Approach

The behavioral analysis-based approach plays a significant role in IoT device security. By monitoring the behavior of IoT devices and identifying abnormal or suspicious behaviors, this approach aims to detect security threats (Zarpelão et al., 2017; Sedjelmaci et al., 2017). It often uses machine learning techniques to model the normal behavior of IoT devices and to detect deviations from this normal behavior (Hodo et al., 2016; Meidan et al., 2017).

This approach is particularly effective at detecting new forms of threats that are not yet known to traditional security systems. This can be attributed to the fact that behavioral analysis focuses on abnormal behaviors rather than specific threat signatures, which allows for the detection of emerging threats and zero-day attacks (Garcia-Teodoro et al., 2009).

However, despite its effectiveness, the behavioral analysis-based approach presents several challenges. One of them is the management of false positives, where normal but unusual behaviors may be wrongly identified as threats. This is particularly problematic in IoT environments where the behaviors of devices can vary greatly (Sedjelmaci et al., 2017; Zarpelão et al., 2017).

Additionally, the behavioral analysis-based approach requires a large volume of data for machine learning to accurately model the normal behavior of IoT devices (Hodo et al., 2016). This can be a challenge in IoT environments where data may be limited or costly to collect.

Lastly, behavioral analysis may be less effective in situations where the normal behavior of IoT devices is difficult to define or model. This may be due to the diversity and complexity of IoT devices and applications, as well as the rapid evolution of IoT technology (Meidan et al., 2017).

Overall, while the behavioral analysis-based approach presents significant advantages for IoT device security, it also requires careful management of the associated challenges to maximize its effectiveness.

3.2.4 Cryptography-Based Approach

The cryptography-based approach is a commonly used method for securing communications in the field of the Internet of Things (IoT). It involves the use of various cryptographic techniques, such as data encryption, device authentication, non-repudiation, and data integrity. These mechanisms play an important role in protecting sensitive information from unauthorized interceptions and modifications (Alaba et al., 2017; Makhdoom et al., 2018).

A major advantage of this approach is that it offers a high level of security and can ensure the identity of devices and users, which is important for preventing identity theft and "man-in-the-middle" attacks (Patel & Patel, 2016). However, as pointed out by Sicari et al. (2015) and Sadeghi et al. (2015), there are significant challenges associated with the cryptography-based approach.

Firstly, cryptographic techniques can be computationally and energetically costly, which can be a problem for IoT devices that typically have limited resources. Secondly, the management of encryption keys can be complex and require additional infrastructure. These problems can be particularly pronounced in environments where IoT devices are widely deployed and where high energy efficiency is required. Indeed, while the cryptography-based approach offers many advantages in terms of security, it also presents significant challenges that need to be taken into account when designing and implementing IoT security solutions.

3.2.5 Machine Learning-Based Approach

The Machine Learning (ML)-based approach is increasingly being used to enhance the security of IoT networks. It uses machine learning techniques to analyze network traffic, identify abnormal behaviors, and take proactive measures to secure devices (Koroniotis et al., 2019). One of the main advantages of this approach is its ability to evolve and adapt to new threats. By learning from past behaviors and constantly adjusting its models, ML can help to quickly detect unknown or evolving attacks (Meidan et al., 2017).

However, the use of ML in IoT networks also presents challenges. For example, ML algorithms require a large amount of data for learning, which can be difficult for IoT networks that typically have limited resources (Buczak & Guven, 2016). Moreover, ML-based systems can be vulnerable to specific attacks, like data poisoning, where attackers inject malicious data into the learning data stream to deceive the system (Ferdowsi & Saad, 2018).

3.2.6 Synthesis and Identification of Gaps

After examining various IoT security approaches, several gaps and challenges can be identified. The security-by-default approach, while essential, is often inadequate as it does not account for rapid evolutions and advancements in cyber-attacks. Moreover, it may overlook user behavior and network dynamics. The network management-based approach, on the other hand, can be complex to implement and manage, particularly for large IoT networks. It is also vulnerable to human errors and internal attacks. The behavioral analysis-based approach is useful for detecting anomalies and suspicious behaviors, but it can also generate a high number of false positives and negatives. Finally, while the ML-based approach is promising for proactive threat detection, it requires a large amount of data for training and can be vulnerable to specific attacks.

These challenges indicate a need for an integrated and holistic approach to IoT security that combines the advantages of these methods while mitigating their limitations. It is in this context that we propose our approach, which combines spatial network type Voronoï diagrams, network centrality, and machine learning-enabled blockchain to enhance IoT security in smart cities.

In the upcoming sections, we will discuss the principles and foundations of our proposed approach, describing the key components and interactions among them.

3.3 KEY CONCEPTS OF OUR APPROACH

3.3.1 Spatial Network Type Voronoï Diagrams

Voronoï diagrams are a computational geometry tool that models the spatial distribution of objects and entities in a plane or multidimensional space. Spatial network type Voronoï diagrams are a variant of these diagrams that incorporate the topological and geometric constraints of communication networks.

We have used Voronoï diagrams in various applications to facilitate spatial planning and analysis. In a study (Mabrouk et al., 2017), a new planning approach for the transport of hazardous materials in urban environments was proposed. It uses Voronoï spatial modeling to assess the proximity of vulnerable areas to transport routes, thus minimizing the risks and damages associated with these materials. In another publication (Mabrouk, Boulmakoul, & Bielli, 2009), the Voronoï diagram is used to assess geographic accessibility in the context of transport planning. This study proposes a method based on fuzzy arithmetic and graph theory to assign each Voronoï generator to its nearest nodes in a real spatial network. Moreover, a distributed architecture based on the analysis of spatial risks and Voronoï spatial accessibility was proposed to ensure pedestrian safety in urban areas (Mabrouk & Boulmakoul, 2022). This work provides a mobile platform guiding pedestrians to the safest routes away from dangerous areas. Finally, in the context of the COVID-19 pandemic, a smart geospatial strategy using Voronoï diagrams was put forward (Mabrouk & Boulmakoul, 2022). It aims to help decision-makers and citizens navigate safely during partial lockdown periods, providing spatial information about infected places, proximity to these places, and safety levels of different areas.

In the context of smart cities and IoT networks, spatial network type Voronoï diagrams have been used to analyze and optimize various aspects of wireless sensor network performance. Different approaches using Voronoï diagrams have been explored to improve IoT network performances.

Abdallah and Val (2020) proposed a hybridization between the Voronoï diagram and the genetic algorithm to maximize the coverage of a region of interest in IoT data collection networks. Their method generates initial solutions for IoT object positioning and improves them to maximize the overall coverage of the region. Wan et al. (2019) highlighted challenges related to processing a large amount of data in real time in IoT deployments. They proposed an energy and time-efficient multidimensional data indexing scheme, using the Voronoï diagram to minimize average energy consumption and query response time. Razzaghi and Babaie (2022) presented a Voronoï diagram-based method to detect selfish behaviors in IoT networks, potentially caused by energy depletion or resource constraints. Tang et al. (2019) proposed a deployment algorithm for 3D sensor networks based on the Voronoï diagram, aiming to maximize the coverage of the surveillance area and improve data security. Adhinugraha et al. (2022, 2021) used the Voronoï diagram to ensure fault tolerance in IoT mesh networks and to identify backup gateways in case of primary gateway failure. Finally, Eledlebi et al. (2018) developed a Voronoï diagram-based algorithm for the efficient deployment of wireless sensor networks in obstacle-rich indoor environments, demonstrating rapid convergence to a fully connected network with low deployment costs.

These works demonstrate the importance of Voronoï diagrams in optimizing IoT sensor networks, addressing challenges such as coverage, data indexing, detection of selfish behaviors, data security, and fault tolerance.

3.3.2 Network Centrality

Network centrality, a fundamental concept in graph theory and social network analysis, allows the measurement of the importance of nodes in a network. Several centrality measures have been proposed, such as degree centrality, closeness centrality, betweenness centrality, and Eigenvector centrality. These measures can be essential in identifying critical IoT devices, security gateways, and data centers within the context of smart cities and IoT networks.

In the context of IoT security, network centrality can assist in identifying the network's vulnerable points and deploying appropriate security measures. For example, a node with high betweenness centrality could be a key control point in the network. Its compromise could have a major impact on the entire network. Likewise, a node with a high degree of centrality could be an important IoT device that communicates with a large number of other devices, and its protection must be prioritized.

These centrality measures have been exploited in various recent research. For instance, Peng et al. (2020) found that using the largest

Eigenvector centrality improves the robustness of cyber-physical systems. Similarly, Nigam et al. (2022) introduced a new centrality measure, local closeness centrality, to enhance forwarding in opportunistic IoT social networks.

In a study conducted by Godquin et al. (2019, 2020), device capabilities were used to model an IoT network as a weighted graph. The most suitable location for a security service was identified using dominating sets and graph weights, thereby increasing network security.

Ahmad et al. (2023) also used centrality measures to identify influential spreaders and vulnerable IoT devices in the context of green smart cities. They highlighted the critical role of static devices in the IoT environment and the need to protect them against malware attacks.

Network centrality can also be used to optimize network topology and improve network resilience against attacks. By identifying and fortifying critical nodes, the network can become more robust against targeted attacks. Moreover, network centrality can contribute to designing fault tolerance and disaster recovery mechanisms, ensuring better resource distribution and greater network resilience.

3.3.3 Machine Learning-Enabled Blockchain

Recent research in the field of Internet of Things (IoT) security has explored the use of blockchain and machine learning to address several security issues. Blockchain is a distributed ledger technology that ensures transparency, security, and data integrity by recording transactions in a chronological sequence across multiple computers to prevent any data tampering.

In the paper by Dorri et al. (2017), the authors present a blockchain-based approach to enhance security and privacy in IoT networks, particularly for smart home environments. Minoli and Occhiogrosso (2018) also highlight the importance of blockchain in securing IoT applications, while acknowledging that blockchain is only a part of the IoT security solution.

Machine learning, a subfield of artificial intelligence, involves building systems capable of learning from data, identifying patterns, and making decisions with minimal human intervention. Integrating machine learning with blockchain can help overcome some of the data security and privacy challenges in the IoT. For example, machine learning can be used to detect anomalous behaviors and suspicious activities in the IoT network, while blockchain can provide a transparent and immutable audit mechanism to trace these suspicious activities.

Khan and Salah (2018) review the main IoT security issues and present blockchain as a key technology for solving these problems, while Mohanta et al. (2020) examine how machine learning, artificial intelligence, and blockchain can be used to address security issues in the IoT.

However, integrating blockchain and machine learning into IoT is not without challenges, including performance, scalability, and data privacy issues. These challenges are also highlighted by Mohanty et al. (2020), who present a lightweight integrated blockchain model to enhance security and privacy in the IoT, while reducing the computational complexity, bandwidth overhead, and latency associated with using blockchain. Overall, this research underscores the importance and potential of machine learning-enabled blockchain in securing IoT networks, while acknowledging the challenges associated with its use.

3.3.4 Justification of Our Approach

As previously mentioned, our approach combines several techniques to enhance IoT security: spatial network type Voronoï diagrams, network centrality, blockchain, and machine learning. We believe this approach has several advantages over existing methods.

First, the use of spatial network type Voronoï diagrams allows for the identification of critical IoT devices within a network. This enables the prioritization of security resources and focuses defense efforts on the devices that are most important for the network's operation.

Second, network centrality enables the identification of devices that are most important for the communication and connectivity of the network. These devices are often prime targets for attackers and thus require increased protection.

Third, machine learning-enabled blockchain provides a robust and transparent method for data management. It can help prevent man-in-the-middle attacks and ensure data integrity.

By combining these techniques, our approach aims to provide enhanced IoT security and network resilience. Compared to existing approaches, our approach offers greater flexibility and adaptability, which is essential in the dynamic and ever-changing landscape of smart cities.

In the following section, we outline our theoretical and conceptual framework for this approach.

3.4 THEORETICAL AND CONCEPTUAL FRAMEWORK

3.4.1 Principles and Foundations of the Proposed Approach

The approach we propose relies on the combination of three key concepts: spatial network type Voronoï diagrams, network centrality, and machine learning-enabled blockchain. These concepts, although different in their nature and application, can be integrated to provide a comprehensive solution to IoT security challenges in smart cities.

Spatial network type Voronoï diagrams serve to model the topology of the IoT network considering the spatial location of IoT devices. They allow the division of space into regions, each region being associated with a specific IoT device. IoT devices within the same region are assumed to be closer to each other in terms of network connectivity, which can aid in the design of more robust and resilient IoT networks.

Network centrality, on the other hand, enables the identification of critical IoT devices based on their position in the network. Devices with high centrality are generally those that have the most interactions with other devices, and thus, are most likely to be targeted by attacks. Therefore, their protection should be prioritized to enhance the overall network security.

Finally, machine learning-enabled blockchain provides a means to secure data and transactions in IoT environments. Through machine learning, it is possible to enhance blockchain consensus mechanisms, detect and prevent attacks, and ensure data integrity.

These three concepts, when combined, can enable a more comprehensive and holistic IoT security approach. The approach we propose aims to leverage the advantages of these three concepts while mitigating their respective limitations. For instance, while spatial network type Voronoï diagrams and network centrality can aid in the design of more robust networks, they do not directly address issues of data security and privacy. On the other hand, although machine learning-enabled blockchain provides mechanisms to secure data, it does not consider network topology and the position of critical IoT devices for security decision-making. Our approach attempts to fill these gaps by integrating these three concepts into a unified framework.

3.4.2 Key Components and Interactions

The approach we propose consists of several key components that interact with each other to enhance IoT security. These components are:

- Spatial Network Type Voronoï Diagram Model: This model is used to represent the topology of the IoT network. Each IoT device is associated with a region of the Voronoï diagram, and devices within the same region are considered closer in terms of network connectivity. This model can aid in identifying the shortest and most efficient communication paths between IoT devices, which can enhance network robustness and resilience.

- Network Centrality Analysis: This analysis is used to identify critical IoT devices. Devices with high centrality are those that have the most interactions with other devices and, thus, are most likely to be targeted by attacks. Therefore, their protection should be prioritized to enhance the overall network security.

- Machine Learning-Enabled Blockchain: This component is used to secure data and transactions in the IoT network. Through machine learning, it is possible to enhance blockchain consensus mechanisms, detect and prevent attacks, and ensure data integrity.

These components interact with each other to provide a comprehensive IoT security solution. For example, the spatial network type Voronoï diagram model can provide valuable insights for network centrality analysis, which in turn can help prioritize security measures. Similarly, the machine learning-enabled blockchain can utilize information from network centrality analysis to improve its consensus mechanisms and attack detection.

3.4.3 Relationships between Voronoï Diagrams, Network Centrality, and Blockchain

Voronoï diagrams, network centrality, and blockchain are not independent concepts, but are closely related within the context of our approach. Voronoï diagrams provide a spatial representation of the IoT network, which is important for network centrality analysis. By identifying critical IoT devices through centrality analysis, we can then prioritize security measures and adapt blockchain mechanisms accordingly. Additionally, the machine learning-enabled blockchain can use network topology information provided by Voronoï diagrams to improve its consensus mechanisms and attack detection.

Indeed, our approach relies on a tight integration of these three concepts, allowing for the optimization of IoT security in smart cities.

3.4.4 Implementation of the Approach

The implementation of our approach involves several key steps. First, it is necessary to gather information about the IoT network topology and the spatial location of devices. This information can be obtained from various sources, such as network registries, connection logs, and GPS location data.

Once this information is collected, it is used to construct a spatial network type Voronoï diagram. This involves dividing the space into regions, each region being associated with a specific IoT device. IoT devices within the same region are presumed to be closer to each other in terms of network connectivity.

Parallel to the construction of the Voronoï diagram, a network centrality analysis is carried out to identify critical IoT devices. This analysis can be performed using different centrality measures, such as degree centrality, closeness centrality, betweenness centrality, and Eigenvector centrality.

Next, a blockchain is established to secure data and transactions in the IoT network. Machine learning is used to enhance the consensus mechanisms of the blockchain, to detect and prevent attacks, and to ensure data integrity.

Finally, the results of the network centrality analysis and information from the blockchain are used to adapt network management and security mechanisms. This might involve, for example, strengthening the security of critical IoT devices, optimizing communication paths to improve network resilience, and using the blockchain to trace and verify transactions.

3.4.5 Evaluation of the Approach's Effectiveness

Determining the effectiveness of our approach relies on both a quantitative and qualitative evaluation.

On a quantitative level, several measures can be used to evaluate the effectiveness of our approach. These measures might include the number of IoT attacks detected and prevented, a reduction in network latency times, improvement in network resilience, and improvement in data integrity. For instance, a significant decrease in the number of successful IoT attacks following the implementation of our approach would be a positive indicator of its effectiveness. Additionally, our approach's ability to maintain acceptable network performance, even in the face of disruptions or attacks, would indicate increased network resilience.

From a qualitative perspective, the evaluation of our approach's effectiveness might be based on criteria such as the ease of use of the system, user satisfaction, the system's ability to adapt to changes in the IoT environment, and the system's response to the specific needs of smart cities. User surveys, interviews with network administrators, and case studies could be used to gather data on these aspects.

Lastly, the cost of implementing our approach should also be considered in evaluating its effectiveness. This includes costs associated with deploying and maintaining IoT devices, installing and managing the blockchain, performing network centrality analysis, and constructing Voronoï diagrams. These costs should be compared to the potential benefits of our approach, such as improved security, reduced network latency times, and increased network resilience. A cost-effective approach would be one that provides a satisfactory level of security and performance for an acceptable cost.

3.5 METHODOLOGIES AND TECHNIQUES

3.5.1 Identification of Critical IoT Devices

Identifying critical IoT devices in the network is an important step towards improving IoT security. Critical devices are those that have a significant role in the overall operation of the network, either because of their strategic position in the network topology or because of the sensitive nature of the data they handle. The compromise of these devices could have serious consequences for the security and reliability of the entire network.

We propose a two-step method to identify critical IoT devices. The first step involves using spatial network type Voronoï diagrams to model the network topology. These diagrams allow us to divide the network into different regions, each representing an IoT device. By analyzing the shape and size of these regions, we can determine the relative position of each device in the network and its degree of interconnection with other devices.

The second step involves using network centrality to analyze the interactions among devices. The centrality of a device in the network is defined as its ability to facilitate communications among other devices. The higher a device's centrality, the more likely it is to be critical to the operation of the network.

To measure centrality, we use measures such as degree centrality (which counts the number of direct connections of a device), closeness centrality (which measures the average distance of a device to all other devices), and betweenness centrality (which measures the number of times a device acts as an intermediary in communications among other devices).

By combining the information obtained from spatial network type Voronoï diagrams and network centrality analysis, we can identify critical IoT devices that need to be prioritized for protection to enhance network security. This approach allows us not only to take into account the network topology and interactions among devices, but also to consider the specificities of each IoT environment.

3.5.2 Prioritization of Security Measures

Once the critical IoT devices are identified, security measures must be prioritized to maximize the effectiveness of protection efforts. For this, we propose an approach based on evaluating the risks associated with each device and using machine learning-enabled blockchain to make informed decisions on the security measures to implement.

We begin by assessing the risks associated with each critical device, considering several factors, such as the device's vulnerability to attacks, the sensitivity of the data handled, the potential impact of a compromise on the network, and the costs associated with implementing security measures. Risk assessment can be performed using multi-criteria analysis techniques, such as hierarchical analysis or a preferential ranking method.

Next, we use the machine learning-enabled blockchain to analyze the risk information and determine the most appropriate security measures for each critical device. The blockchain offers a decentralized and transparent mechanism for storing and sharing risk information, ensuring that security decisions are made collaboratively and based on reliable data. Machine learning can be used to analyze the data from the blockchain and identify patterns and trends that can help predict potential attacks and design suitable security strategies.

Risk-based security measure prioritization using machine learning-enabled blockchain allows the focus of protection efforts on the most vulnerable critical IoT devices and the optimization of resource use to enhance the security of the entire network.

3.5.3 Designing Resilient Networks

Resilience is a fundamental characteristic of a secure IoT network. It refers to the ability of a system to maintain its operation despite disruptions and to recover quickly after an attack. To create resilient IoT networks, it is necessary to apply the principles of network centrality and spatial network type Voronoï diagrams, as well as blockchain technology.

Network centrality plays an important role in designing resilient networks. By identifying the most important, or "central", nodes in a network, protection and reinforcement efforts can be prioritized. For instance, an IoT device that plays a central role in the network, like a router or a data hub, could be reinforced with additional security measures or duplicated to ensure redundancy.

Spatial network type Voronoï diagrams can also contribute to resilience by helping to optimize the network topology. By dividing the network into cells based on the proximity of IoT devices, the communication distance between devices can be minimized, reducing the possibility of interception or disruption of communications. Moreover, this approach can help identify areas of the network that are vulnerable to attacks and require additional protection.

Finally, blockchain technology can enhance resilience by ensuring transparency and traceability of transactions in the network. By storing all transactions on a blockchain, an immutable and verifiable record of all network activities can be created. This makes it much more challenging for an attacker to alter or falsify data and allows for quick detection of any attack attempt.

Indeed, designing resilient networks is a complex process that involves optimizing network topology, identifying and protecting critical devices, and ensuring complete transparency and traceability of transactions. By combining the principles of network centrality, spatial network type Voronoï diagrams, and blockchain, robust and resilient IoT networks can be created that can withstand attacks and recover quickly in case of disruption.

3.5.4 Detection and Prevention of Attacks

The detection and prevention of attacks is a final essential step in ensuring IoT security. Here again, the combination of machine learning-enabled blockchain, spatial network type Voronoï diagrams, and network centrality offers a powerful methodology to identify abnormal behaviors and quickly intervene to prevent attacks.

Applying spatial network type Voronoï diagrams and network centrality allows observation of communication patterns within the IoT network. This can help identify abnormal or suspicious behaviors that could indicate an attack attempt. For example, an IoT device suddenly sending a large amount of data to another device might be compromised.

Additionally, machine learning-enabled blockchain can enhance attack detection and prevention by providing a reliable source of information on device behavior. Machine learning can be used to analyze blockchain data and develop normal behavior models for each IoT device. These models can then be used to identify abnormal behaviors and trigger security alerts.

Furthermore, the blockchain can provide an incident response mechanism that allows for the quick isolation of compromised devices and prevents the attack from spreading. In case of abnormal behavior detection, the suspect device can be automatically isolated from the network until it is verified.

Indeed, the combination of these technologies and methodologies allows for the construction of a robust attack detection and prevention system, thus enhancing the overall security of IoT systems in smart cities.

3.5.5 Comparison of Our Approach with Existing Methods

Our proposed approach stands out from other methods by its use of a combination of spatial network type Voronoï diagrams, network centrality, and machine learning-enabled blockchain. This approach is highly effective in enhancing IoT security, network resilience, and data management (Table 3.1).

Our approach offers a holistic perspective on IoT security, by combining several aspects of different existing approaches. Unlike the default security approach, we don't focus solely on preventing vulnerabilities during design and manufacture, but also incorporate techniques for detecting and preventing attacks.

Compared to the network management approach, our approach goes further by using not only network monitoring to detect suspicious activities, but also blockchain to ensure transparency and traceability of transactions.

Our approach stands out from behavioral analysis in that we don't just use machine learning techniques to detect abnormal behaviors, but also to identify trends and anomalies in the data.

Unlike the cryptography-based approach, we don't solely rely on cryptography to secure communications between IoT devices. Instead, we use a combination of network centrality, Voronoï diagrams, and blockchain to

TABLE 3.1 Comparison of our approach with existing methods for IoT security

Methods	IoT Security	Network Resilience	Data Management
Our Approach	Uses network centrality, Voronoï diagrams, and blockchain with machine learning to identify and protect critical devices and detect and prevent attacks.	Uses a combination of network centrality, Voronoï diagrams, and blockchain to design resilient networks.	Employs blockchain to ensure transparency and traceability of transactions, and machine learning to analyze data and identify trends and anomalies.
Default Security	Prevents vulnerabilities from the design and manufacturing stage, uses secure communication protocols, and implements strong authentication and encryption measures.	Not specified.	Not specified.
Network Management	Monitors and controls network activities to identify and block suspicious or malicious activities.	May help detect and prevent real-time attacks.	Not specified.
Behavioral Analysis	Monitors IoT device behavior to identify abnormal or suspicious behaviors.	Not specified.	Uses machine learning techniques to model the normal behavior of IoT devices and detect deviations from this normal behavior.
Cryptography	Uses cryptography techniques to secure communications between IoT devices.	Not specified.	Protects sensitive data against unauthorized interception and modifications.
Machine Learning	Uses machine learning techniques to detect and prevent attacks on IoT networks.	Not specified.	Analyzes network traffic and identifies abnormal behaviors.

design resilient networks that can maintain their operation despite disturbances and recover quickly after an attack.

Finally, compared to the machine learning-based approach, our approach isn't limited to the use of machine learning techniques for attack detection and prevention. We also use blockchain to ensure transaction transparency and traceability, which enhances data security and reduces the possibility of attacks.

Furthermore, the default security approach is good for IoT security but weak in data management. Network management is good for network resilience, but only average in IoT security and data management. Behavioral analysis is good for data management but weak in network resilience. Cryptography excels in IoT security and data management, but is weak in network resilience (Figure 3.1).

The machine learning-based approach is good in all domains, but not excellent. On the other hand, our approach (Voronoï + Centrality + Blockchain-ML) is excellent in all aspects, demonstrating superior performance in IoT security, network resilience, and data management.

Indeed, our approach leverages the strengths of each of these existing methods while compensating for their weaknesses, enabling us to provide a more comprehensive and resilient IoT security solution.

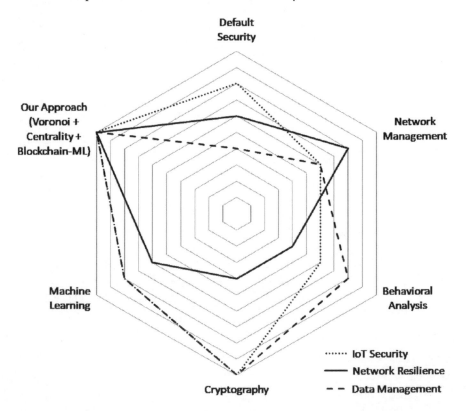

FIGURE 3.1   Comparison and evaluation of approaches

3.6 APPLICATIONS AND IMPLICATIONS FOR VARIOUS SECTORS

3.6.1 Intelligent Transportation

In the field of intelligent transportation, our approach can be used to enhance the security of communications between connected vehicles and transportation infrastructures. For example, Voronoï diagrams based on spatial networks can be utilized to identify congestion areas and critical points in the transportation network. Network centrality can then be employed to determine the importance of each vehicle or infrastructure within the network, while blockchain, enabled by machine learning, can secure communications and transactions among them.

Applying our approach in the context of intelligent transportation can yield several benefits. It can enhance the resilience of the transportation network against attacks and disruptions by enabling rapid and accurate identification of critical devices and ensuring secure communications. Moreover, it can facilitate better traffic management and congestion reduction by providing valuable insights into the network's structure and operation. Finally, it can contribute to user trust in intelligent transportation systems by guaranteeing data confidentiality and integrity.

3.6.2 Smart Energy Management

In the domain of smart energy management, our approach can be applied to enhance the security of energy distribution networks. Voronoï diagrams can aid in identifying critical elements of the network, such as substations or transformers, which require increased protection. Additionally, network centrality can help understand the potential impact of an attack or malfunction on the rest of the network. Lastly, blockchain, enabled by machine learning, can be employed to secure energy transactions, for instance, in the context of microgrids or distributed renewable energy systems.

Utilizing this approach in the field of smart energy management can lead to improved resilience and security of energy distribution networks. It can also facilitate more efficient energy management, such as better coordination between energy producers and consumers. Furthermore, ensuring the confidentiality and integrity of energy transactions can enhance user confidence in smart energy management systems.

3.6.3 Smart Healthcare

In the domain of smart healthcare, our approach can be utilized to enhance the security of connected medical devices and electronic health systems. Voronoï diagrams can aid in identifying critical devices or systems that require increased protection. Network centrality can help understand the potential impact of an attack or malfunction on the rest of the healthcare system. Lastly, blockchain, enabled by machine learning, can be employed to secure healthcare data and transactions among different healthcare stakeholders.

Applying our approach in the field of smart healthcare can result in a significant improvement in the security and resilience of electronic health systems and connected medical devices. It can also contribute to the confidentiality and integrity of healthcare data, which is important for patient and healthcare professional trust in digital health technologies. Additionally, it can facilitate better coordination and management of healthcare, providing valuable insights into the structure and operation of the healthcare system.

3.6.4 Other Sectors

Our approach can also be applied in other domains such as public safety, smart agriculture, or intelligent water management. In all these cases, it can help identify critical devices or systems, understand their roles and impact on the rest of the network, and secure communications and transactions among them. Potential benefits include enhanced network resilience and security, improved resource management, and increased trust in IoT technologies.

3.7 DISCUSSION AND IMPLICATIONS

3.7.1 Advantages of the Proposed Approach

The approach presented in this paper offers several significant advantages. Firstly, it allows for more precise and effective identification of critical IoT devices in smart cities, which can help prioritize security efforts and design appropriate protection measures. Secondly, it promotes the design of resilient IoT networks that can withstand and quickly recover from attacks or malfunctions. Thirdly, it facilitates the detection and prevention of attacks through the use of machine learning-enabled blockchain technology.

3.7.2 Implications for Researchers, Practitioners, and Decision-Makers

This approach has important implications for researchers, practitioners, and decision-makers in the field of IoT security for smart cities. For researchers, it provides a new framework for understanding and studying the security of IoT networks. For practitioners, it offers tools and techniques that can be used to enhance the security of the IoT systems they design, develop, or manage. For decision-makers, it highlights the importance of security in the development of smart cities and can inform the creation of policies and regulations in this area.

3.7.3 Directions for Future Research and Experimentation

While this paper proposes a theoretical approach to enhance IoT security in smart cities, further research is needed to test and refine this approach in practice. For example, experimental studies could be conducted to evaluate the effectiveness of the approach in different contexts and for different types of IoT networks. Additionally, research could be conducted to explore the challenges and potential solutions associated with the implementation of the approach, such as privacy and data protection challenges related to the use of machine learning-enabled blockchain technology.

3.8 CONCLUSION AND PERSPECTIVE

This paper has presented an innovative approach to enhance IoT security in smart cities by combining spatial network type Voronoï diagrams, network centrality, and machine learning-enabled blockchain technology. The approach aims to identify critical IoT devices, prioritize security measures, design resilient networks, and detect and prevent attacks. Examples of applications and implications for various sectors of smart cities have been discussed, highlighting the potential of the approach to improve the security and resilience of IoT ecosystems.

While the proposed approach offers many advantages, it also comes with challenges and limitations. For instance, constructing Voronoï diagrams and calculating network centrality can be complex and require significant computational resources, while the use of machine learning-enabled blockchain raises privacy and data protection concerns. However, with proper development and implementation, these challenges can be effectively managed.

The approach presented in this paper provides a fresh perspective on IoT security in smart cities and opens up numerous avenues for future research and experimentation. For instance, further research could be conducted to test and refine the approach in various contexts and for different types of IoT networks. Additionally, research could explore other techniques and methodologies that can be integrated into the approach to further enhance the security of IoT networks.

Indeed, the approach presented in this paper represents a significant contribution to IoT security research for smart cities. It offers a solid theoretical and conceptual framework, as well as practical methodologies and techniques, to improve the security and resilience of IoT networks. It also paves the way for further research and experimentation in this important field.

REFERENCES

Abdallah, W., & Val, T. (2020). Genetic-Voronoï algorithm for coverage of IoT data collection networks. In *2020 30th International Conference on Computer Theory and Applications (ICCTA)* (pp. 16–22). IEEE. https://doi.org/10.1109/ICCTA52020.2020.9477675.

Adat, V., & Gupta, B. B. (2018). Security in Internet of Things: Issues, challenges, taxonomy, and architecture. *Telecommunication Systems*, 67(3), 423–441. https://doi.org/10.1007/s11235-017-0345-9.

Adhinugraha, K., Rahayu, W., Hara, T., & Taniar, D. (2021). Backup gateways for IoT mesh network using order-k hops Voronoi diagram. *World Wide Web*, 24(3), 955–970. https://doi.org/10.1007/s11280-020-00852-5.

Adhinugraha, K., Rahayu, W., Hara, T., & Taniar, D. (2022). Measuring fault tolerance in IoT mesh networks using Voronoi diagram. *Journal of Network and Computer Applications*, 199, 103297. https://doi.org/10.1016/j.jnca.2021.103297.

Ahmad, A., Ahmad, T., Ahmad, M., Kumar, C., Alenezi, F., & Nour, M. (2023). A complex network-based approach for security and governance in the smart green city. *Expert Systems with Applications*, 214, 119094.

Alaba, F. A., Othman, M., Hashem, I. A. T., & Alotaibi, F. (2017). Internet of Things security: A survey. *Journal of Network and Computer Applications*, 88, 10–28.

Al-Fuqaha, M., Guizani, M., Mohammadi, M., Mohammadi, A., & Ayyash, M. (2015). Internet of Things: A survey on enabling technologies, protocols, and applications. In *IEEE Communications Surveys & Tutorials*, 17(4), 2347–2376, Fourth quarter 2015. https://doi.org/10.1109/COMST.2015.2444095.

Alrawais, A., Alhothaily, A., Hu, C., & Cheng, X. (2017). Fog computing for the internet of things: Security and privacy issues. *IEEE Internet Computing*, 21(2), 34–42.

Buczak, A. L., & Guven, E. (2016). A survey of data mining and machine learning methods for cyber security intrusion detection. *IEEE Communications Surveys and Tutorials*, 18(2), 1153–1176.

Can, O., & Sahingoz, O. K. (2015). A survey of intrusion detection systems in wireless sensor networks. In *2015 6th International Conference on Modeling, Simulation, and Applied Optimization (ICMSAO)* (pp. 1–6). https://doi.org /10.1109/ICMSAO.2015.7152200.

Dorri, A., Kanhere, S. S., Jurdak, R., & Gauravaram, P. (2017). Blockchain for IoT security and privacy: The case study of a smart home. In *2017 IEEE International Conference on Pervasive Computing and Communications Workshops (PerCom Workshops)* (pp. 618–623). IEEE. https://doi.org/10 .1109/PERCOMW.2017.7917634.

Eledlebi, K., Ruta, D., Saffre, F., AlHammadi, Y., & Isakovic, A. F. (2018). Voronoi-based indoor deployment of mobile sensors network with obstacles. In *2018 IEEE 3rd International Workshops on Foundations and Applications of Self* Systems (FAS*W)* (pp. 20–21). IEEE. https://doi.org/10.1109/FAS-W.2018 .00019.

Ferdowsi, A., & Saad, W. (2018). Deep learning-based dynamic watermarking for secure signal authentication in the Internet of Things. In *2018 IEEE International Conference on Communications (ICC)* (pp. 1–6). IEEE.

Frustaci, M., Pace, P., Aloi, G., & Fortino, G. (2018). Evaluating critical security issues of the IoT world: Present and future challenges. *IEEE Internet of Things Journal*, 5(4), 2483–2495.

Garcia-Teodoro, P., Diaz-Verdejo, J., Maciá-Fernández, G., & Vázquez, E. (2009). Anomaly-based network intrusion detection: Techniques, systems and challenges. *Computers and Security*, 28(1–2), 18–28.

Godquin, T., Barbier, M., Gaber, C., Grimault, J. -L., & Le Bars, J. -M. (2019). Placement optimization of IoT security solutions for edge computing based on graph theory. In *2019 IEEE 38th International Performance Computing and Communications Conference (IPCCC)* (pp. 1–7). IEEE.

Godquin, T., Barbier, M., Gaber, C., Grimault, J.-L., & Le Bars, J.-M. (2020). Applied graph theory to security: A qualitative placement of security solutions within IoT networks. *Journal of Information Security and Applications*, 55, 102640.

Hodo, E., Bellekens, X., Hamilton, A., Dubouilh, P. L., Iorkyase, E., Tachtatzis, C., & Atkinson, R. (2016). Threat analysis of IoT networks using artificial neural network intrusion detection system. In *2016 International Symposium on Networks, Computers and Communications (ISNCC)* (pp. 1–6). IEEE.

Khan, M. A., & Salah, K. (2018). IoT security: Review, blockchain solutions, and open challenges. *Future Generation Computer Systems*, 82, 395–411. ISSN 0167-739X. https://doi.org/10.1016/j.future.2017.11.022.

Kolias, C., Kambourakis, G., Stavrou, A., & Voas, J. (2017). DDoS in the IoT: Mirai and other botnets. *Computer*, 50(7), 80–84.

Koroniotis, N., Moustafa, N., Sitnikova, E., & Slay, J. (2019). Towards the development of realistic botnet dataset in the Internet of Things for network forensic analytics: Bot-IoT dataset. *Future Generation Computer Systems*, 100, 779–796.

Mabrouk, A., & Boulmakoul, A. (2022a). Safest trajectories for pedestrians using distributed architecture based on spatial risk analysis and Voronoï spatial accessibility. In *Smart Trajectories*. https://doi.org/10.1201/9781003255635 -16.

Mabrouk, A., & Boulmakoul, A. (2022b). Smart COVID-19 GeoStrategies using spatial network Voronoï diagrams. In *Machine Learning and Deep Learning in Medical Data Analytics and Healthcare Applications*. https://doi.org/10 .1201/9781003226147-14.

Mabrouk, A., Boulmakoul, A., & Bielli, M. (2009). Fuzzy spatial network Voronoï diagram: A spatial decision support for transportation planning. *International Journal of Services Sciences*, 2(3/4). https://doi.org/10.1504/ IJSSCI.2009.026542.

Mabrouk, A., Boulmakoul, L., Karim, A., & Lbath, A. (2017). Safest and short-est itineraries for transporting hazardous materials using split points of Voronoï spatial diagrams based on spatial modeling of vulnerable zones. *Procedia Computer Science*, 109. https://doi.org/10.1016/j.procs.2017.05.311.

Makhdoom, I., Abolhasan, M., Lipman, J., Liu, R. P., & Ni, W. (2018). Anatomy of threats to the Internet of Things. *IEEE Communications Surveys and Tutorials*, 21(2), 1636–1675.

Meidan, Y., Bohadana, M., Shabtai, A., Guarnizo, J. D., Ochoa, M., Tippenhauer, N. O., & Elovici, Y. (2017). ProfilIoT: A machine learning approach for IoT device identification based on network traffic analysis. In *Proceedings of the Symposium on Applied Computing* (pp. 506–509).

Minoli, D., & Occhiogrosso, B. (2018). Blockchain mechanisms for IoT security. *Internet of Things*, 1–2, 1–13. ISSN 2542-6605. https://doi.org/10.1016/j.iot .2018.05.002.

Mohanta, B. K., Jena, D., Satapathy, U., & Patnaik, S. (2020). Survey on IoT secu-rity: Challenges and solution using machine learning, artificial intelligence and blockchain technology. *Internet of Things*, 11, 100227. ISSN 2542-6605. https://doi.org/10.1016/j.iot.2020.100227.

Mohanty, S. N., Ramya, K. C., Rani, S. S., Gupta, D., Shankar, K., Lakshmanaprabu, S. K., & Khanna, A. (2020). An efficient Lightweight integrated Blockchain (ELIB) model for IoT security and privacy. *Future Generation Computer Systems*, 102, 1027–1037. ISSN 0167-739X. https://doi.org/10.1016/j.future .2019.09.050.

Nigam, R., Sharma, D. K., Jain, S., & Srivastava, G. (2022). A local betweenness centrality based forwarding technique for social opportunistic IoT net-works. *Mobile Networks and Applications*, 27(2), 547–562.

Patel, K. K., & Patel, S. M. (2016). Internet of Things-IOT: Definition, charac-teristics, architecture, enabling technologies, application & future chal-lenges. *International Journal of Engineering Science and Computing*, 6(5), 6122–6131.

Peng, H., Liu, C., Zhao, D., Ye, H., Fang, Z., & Wang, W. (2020). Security analysis of CPS systems under different swapping strategies in IoT environments. *IEEE Access*, 8, 63567–63576.

Razzaghi, N., & Babaie, S. (2022). A new selfish thing detection method based on Voronoi diagram for Internet of Things. *Journal of Supercomputing*, 78(6), 8389–8408. https://doi.org/10.1007/s11227-021-04202-8.

Sadeghi, A. R., Wachsmann, C., & Waidner, M. (2015). Security and privacy challenges in industrial Internet of Things. In *2015 52nd ACM/EDAC/IEEE Design Automation Conference (DAC)* (pp. 1–6). IEEE.

Sedjelmaci, H., Senouci, S. M., & Taleb, T. (2017). An efficient intrusion detection framework in cluster-based wireless sensor networks. *IEEE Transactions on Vehicular Technology*, 66(10), 8833–8846.

Sfar, A. R., Natalizio, E., Challal, Y., & Chtourou, Z. (2018). A roadmap for security challenges in the Internet of Things. *Digital Communications and Networks*, 4(2), 118–137.

Sicari, S., Rizzardi, A., Grieco, L. A., & Coen-Porisini, A. (2015). Security, privacy and trust in Internet of Things: The road ahead. *Computer Networks*, 76, 146–164.

Tang, X., Tan, L., Hussain, A., & Wang, M. (2019). Three-dimensional Voronoi diagram–based self-deployment algorithm in IoT sensor networks. *Annals of Telecommunications*, 74(7–8), 517–529. https://doi.org/10.1007/s12243 -018-0686-8.

Wan, S., Zhao, Y., Wang, T., Gu, Z., Abbasi, Q. H., & Choo, K.-K. R. (2019). Multi-dimensional data indexing and range query processing via Voronoi diagram for internet of things. *Future Generation Computer Systems*, 91, 382–391. https://doi.org/10.1016/j.future.2018.08.007.

Zarpelão, B. B., Miani, R. S., Kawakani, C. T., & de Alvarenga, S. C. (2017). A survey of intrusion detection in Internet of Things. *Journal of Network and Computer Applications*, 84, 25–37.

CHAPTER 4

The Combination of Blockchain and the Internet of Things (IoT): Applications, Opportunities, and Challenges for Industry

Taushif Anwar, Ghufran Ahmad Khan,
Zubair Ashraf, Zulfikar Ali Ansari, Rafeeq
Ahmed, and Mourade Azrour

4.1 INTRODUCTION

A blockchain is a form of distributed ledger technology (DLT) that comprises linked blocks containing information. All nodes in the network have access to the same blockchain ledger and database, allowing them to securely track the movement of funds between nodes. Blockchain and smart contracts have been identified as major advancements with the potential to revolutionize every day and business life [1]. Some people have

DOI: 10.1201/9781003438779-4

expressed concerns about the widespread adoption of blockchain technology, believing it to be underdeveloped and too hyped. The remarkable features, efficiency, and durability of this technology present a compelling prospect for many individuals. Its application should be customized to meet the needs of its users, and several insurance companies are actively investigating the potential benefits of integrating blockchain technology into their sector [2].

Over a decade ago, the first utilization of blockchain emerged, which entailed a shared database for transactions within a decentralized network. This implies that all individuals can store all transactions in one centralized location [3]. Distributed computing could be a beneficial option for individuals who are unwilling to rely on a single person or organization. They can collaborate autonomously without requiring assistance from anyone else.

Over the past few years, there has been a notable surge in the adoption of Internet of Things (IoT) devices worldwide. The reasons behind this rise include the need for faster and more efficient production methods in the global market, the desire to improve military capabilities, and the trend towards creating "smart" environments like smart cities, smart factories, and smart homes. Despite the numerous benefits offered by Internet of Things (IoT) devices, they also bring about certain drawbacks. These drawbacks encompass the generation of large amounts of data, considerable energy usage, and vulnerabilities related to trust issues arising from centralized control by an administrator who holds the power to manipulate or disrupt the system. IoT devices gather data about themselves and their surroundings, which they send to a central server. However, blockchain technology has emerged as a way to address these potential weaknesses and risks by enabling secure and trustworthy data exchange between IoT devices or with a cloud server.

Nakamoto, the individual behind Bitcoin, introduced the first cryptocurrency that utilizes DLT, commonly known as blockchain. Since then, this innovative technology has found its place in the Internet of Things (IoT) sector, enabling internet-connected smart devices to utilize a secure, immutable, and auditable network. Blockchain functions as a decentralized ledger, ensuring the safety, verification, and recording of all peer-to-peer transactions in a swift, secure, and transparent manner. One of the key benefits of employing blockchain technology is that it enables two parties to engage in secure online transactions without the need for a trusted middleman. Consequently, transaction costs are reduced compared to traditional methods that rely on such intermediaries.

The number of connected IoT devices is expected to reach 16.44 billion by 2025 and 25.44 billion by 2030, driven by the increasing reliance on smart devices [4]. This growth is set to have a significant impact on the IoT market, and blockchain technology is predicted to play a transformative role. Several vendors are currently working on developing new platforms, tools, and techniques to leverage the security and transparency advantages of blockchain. However, blockchain platforms alone are unable to handle the vast amount of data generated. As a result, in many cases, a separate data warehouse is needed to store the extensive data that cannot be directly accommodated on the blockchain platform. This data warehouse can take the form of a cloud data warehouse or a traditional central database management system. Cloud data warehouses are particularly favored due to their scalability and advanced functionalities. Notably, there has been an increase in the development of blockchain applications and platforms that leverage cloud storage solutions.

4.2 LITERATURE REVIEW BASED ON THE COMBINATION OF BLOCKCHAIN AND THE INTERNET OF THINGS (IOT)

Kamalendu Pal et al. [1] introduced a blockchain-driven framework for IoT applications, showcasing the utilization of distributed data management to facilitate transaction services in a supply chain network involving multiple parties within the textile industry. They proposed a hybrid architecture for enterprise information systems that integrates IoT applications with a blockchain-based distributed ledger, enabling transaction services within a global apparel industry network that involves multiple parties. Furthermore, they presented a research proposal discussing the potential impact of blockchain technology on important components of IoT systems and laying the foundation for future research endeavors.

Manojkumar Vivekanandan et al. [2] introduced BIDAPSCA5G, an innovative authentication protocol for IoT devices in smart city applications. This protocol takes advantage of 5G technology and is built upon a Blockchain framework. It efficiently manages the registration of IoT devices by implementing a private blockchain. Notably, it offers supplementary functionalities like authentication based on device location, registration and revocation of Internet of Things Devices (IoTD) using blockchain, device-level anonymity for IoTDs, thorough security analysis utilizing the Random Oracle Model (ROM), and informal security analysis.

Ashutosh Dhar Dwivedi et al. [3] investigate the integration of blockchain technology into a network of healthcare applications. Their aim is to ensure the secure and confidential use of patient health data in order to provide important alerts to verified healthcare providers. The study highlights the main challenges faced by the IoT and blockchain in achieving effective collaboration. The proposed approach combines blockchain and IoT to address most privacy and security concerns, taking into account the limitations of IoTDs with limited resources. Additionally, the authors introduce a blockchain-based security solution that is specifically designed for certain IoT systems, including remote patient monitoring systems.

Ashutosh Dhar Dwivedi et al. [4] tackled the issue of network scalability by implementing a decentralized blockchain network. They utilized the Raft consensus algorithm to enhance the blockchain's capacity for handling transactions. Privacy emerges as a major concern in Internet of Things (IoT) networks. The scholarly paper explored the potential applications and industrial utilization of IoTDs enabled by 5G technology, spanning various areas such as supply chain management, e-voting, industry 5.0, and smart homes. The authors also identified significant hurdles in integrating blockchain and IoT devices, including the need for scalable storage and throughput, network scalability, and privacy. They conducted a thorough examination of each proposed solution aimed at overcoming these challenges and successfully merging the two systems.

Naser Hossein Motlagh et al. [5] investigated the diverse applications of IoT across all stages of the energy supply chain, including energy generation, energy grids, and end-use sectors. Their objective was to offer a comprehensive understanding of how IoT contributes to optimizing the energy system for energy policymakers, economists, and managers. The researchers also analyzed the obstacles involved in implementing IoT in the energy industry, which encompassed areas such as managing big data, resolving connectivity issues, addressing uncertainty, integrating subsystems, ensuring security and privacy, and meeting the energy requirements of IoT systems. Moreover, they underscored the importance of standardization and architectural design within this context.

Norah Saleh Alghamdi et al. [6] proposed the utilization of K-means clustering and linear network coding in WSN with IoT devices enabled by blockchain technology. The K-means clustering method is employed to choose cluster heads based on factors such as energy usage and proximity to the base station. The authors assessed the proposed model by considering metrics such as the number of active nodes, packet delivery ratio, throughput, energy consumption, and dependability.

Rajasekhar Chaganti et al. [7] created a smart-farm security monitoring system that utilizes cloud technology. Its main purposes are to monitor sensor anomalies and device status effectively and to prevent security attacks by analyzing behavioral patterns. Additionally, they incorporated a blockchain-based smart contract application to securely store information about security anomalies and ensure that similar attacks are avoided in neighboring farms.

Marah R. Bataineh et al. [8] introduced a technique that addresses the challenges arising from limited IoT resources when implementing blockchain mining in IoT systems. The researchers suggested an approach that combines an Ethereum Blockchain infrastructure with a rich-thin client IoT model. The success of this approach hinges on the efficient distribution of workload among the available resources. To improve the system's overall performance, resource utilization, data privacy, and security, the team devised a collaborative healthcare management solution known as ERTCA. This solution leverages the integration of IoT and blockchain technologies.

Ali Hassan Sodhro et al. [9] put forth a preliminary secure framework and algorithm for an IoT system that incorporates blockchain technology. Moreover, they employ an advanced security algorithm based on blockchain for IoT systems, aiming to guarantee both security and efficiency throughout the entire process. The algorithm they propose makes use of a mechanism that manages random initial and master keys, effectively safeguarding sensitive industrial environments from eavesdropping and unauthorized access.

Rajani Singh et al. [10] introduced an IoT blockchain system that relies on sensors to monitor and trace the movement of medicines throughout the supply chain. The utilization of blockchain and IoT sensors has a substantial impact on supply chain management. However, it also presents novel security concerns for IoTDs with limited resources and challenges related to the scalability of blockchain in handling the data generated by IoT sensors.

4.3 APPLICATIONS OF BLOCKCHAIN AND THE INTERNET OF THINGS (IOT)

4.3.1 The Combination of Blockchain and the Internet of Things (IoT) for AI (Artificial Intelligence)

The essential components of AI technology include data, algorithms, and computing power. Effective algorithm training requires a significant amount of computing power, which in turn requires a large volume of data for building classification models. In the current era of big data, data can be obtained from a variety of sources, such as sensors, IoTDs, and social media platforms. However, this poses the risk of multiple parties owning the same data, which can cause various issues[11]. For instance, relying solely on data from a single source or stakeholder to train AI models can be expensive or unfeasible. Moreover, consolidating data processing in one central location can pose significant risks in case of any mishaps or failures. Furthermore, data from multiple sources can be disorganized and of varying quality, which can make it challenging to create effective models[12].

4.3.1.1 Data Sharing

To be effective, AI requires a significant amount of data, particularly high-quality data that can improve its classification results. However, trust can be difficult to establish among those who own the training data. The process of verifying and validating data can be challenging, and there may be instances where individuals purposely provide malicious data for various reasons. Blockchain has been utilized in the past to address similar trust issues in data markets. This new platform enables communication and collaboration between providers of IoT and AI solutions. It facilitates user registration, data search, purchasing, payment, and feedback submission via a smart contract. By utilizing a Private Data Center (PDC), users have control over their data and can make informed decisions on how they want to utilize it.

4.3.1.2 Preserving Privacy

Maintaining privacy is a significant concern, as users risk compromising their information when sharing data. The acquisition of personal information from a large corporation is problematic since it can be exploited.

Deep LinQ, a distributed, multi-layer ledger, has the potential to safeguard shared data privacy. However, blockchain technology, despite its potential utility, is not suitable for storing medical information due to its need for efficiency and complete decentralization. The branch layer of Deep LinQ is tailored to meet the requirements of its users.

4.3.1.3 Decentralized Intelligence

Amidst the speedy expansion of the IoT, a great deal of information about it has been generated. An AI service such as Siri can assist in uncovering patterns and models from the vast amount of IoT data available. The proliferation of IoT and edge computing devices necessitates the sharing of data to facilitate the prediction and analysis of future events. To achieve this, individuals must initiate actions like intelligent monitoring, cross-regional monitoring, and data sharing.

4.3.2 The Combination of Blockchain and the Internet of Things (IoT) for Environments

The extensive utilization of telecommunications technology has led to a wide array of products and services being employed by individuals and businesses. The consequences of these shifts in telecommunications services are far-reaching and affect multiple areas, including data measurement, fax transmission, teleconferencing, computer-to-computer communication, software-defined networking (SDN), and electronic healthcare. Moreover, the Telecommunications IoT has emerged as a significant market in recent years, with advanced communication systems such as satellite communications, 5G technology, and mobile communications incorporating this technology. One such system is the Smart IoV, which benefits from improved communication and connectivity between these technologies. As the telecommunications IoT market continues to evolve, there is growing interest in the digital changes that will occur and how telecommunications can facilitate them. The IoT allows for the effortless connection of smart devices without human intervention [13], while the Wireless Body Area Network (WBAN) consists of a set of intelligent devices that communicate independently with each other. Data is collected by mobile devices and then sent to access points, facilitating communication between devices.

4.3.3 The Combination of Blockchain and the Internet of Things (IoT) for Intelligent Agriculture

The blockchain consists of multiple nodes, each of which maintains its own distributed ledger. These ledgers can be accessed and updated simultaneously by many nodes, which collectively maintain the system. Because all nodes share the same ledger, there is no need for intermediaries to verify transactions, making the system decentralized and secure. Blockchain technology can be applied in various areas such as food, raw materials, music, data, and apps. Once a transaction is added to the ledger, it cannot be removed or altered due to encryption. This makes the blockchain a trustworthy and reliable source of information in the network [14].

4.3.4 The Combination of Blockchain and the Internet of Things (IoT) for Smart Grid

In the past, individuals who owned small businesses and homes couldn't purchase the necessary equipment to produce electricity, so they relied on a nearby power plant that transmitted electricity through the power grid and paid for the service. However, with the emergence of new technology, obtaining and disseminating electricity has become more accessible and cost-effective through automation and alternative energy sources such as solar, wave, and geothermal power. Nevertheless, the process has changed significantly from before [15–18].

4.3.5 The Combination of Blockchain and Internet of Things (IoT) for Smart Homes and Other Appliances

The Internet of Things (IoT) has become increasingly popular as more devices are integrated into our daily lives, leading to economic growth. However, concerns about the long-term security of the country have been raised. To address this, it is suggested that each IoT node should have more power rather than relying on a central server or person.

The IoT allows mobile devices to be connected and controlled remotely through the internet, with sensors providing information about their environment. Smart home devices like TVs, washing machines, air conditioning units, and lights are commonly used to monitor homes and appliances. IoT networks constantly exchange data, which is stored in a database on a server or the cloud, with no human involvement. This data can be sent to private blockchain ledgers through the IoT, ensuring tamper-proof transactions that are visible to others. People can also access the IoT and blockchain networks using this approach.

Most published works center around the application of smart contracts within an IoT framework based on blockchain technology, aiming to guarantee the security and privacy of devices. The proposed methods are both lightweight and decentralized, removing the requirement for cooperation in order to maintain device security. Essentially, the articles elucidate the process by which multiple entities can mutually commit to written agreements [19–23].

Ethereum is a type of blockchain that operates in a decentralized manner, serving as an open-source platform and facilitating the implementation of smart contracts. Its primary purpose is to facilitate the creation of smart contracts that execute specific tasks on the internet. Ethereum is widely regarded as the best blockchain platform and can be applied to various use cases, such as smart homes. For example, multiple individuals can use the same devices and services in a smart home. In order for this to happen, it is necessary for all devices to establish a connection with a central IoT hub, which will bring them together and integrate their functionalities. It is essential to record each transaction quickly on the blockchain for universal access. Moreover, there is a need for a smart home IoT hub to store tokens for future use.

4.3.6 The Combination of Blockchain and Internet of Things (IoT) for Smart Transportation

Over the past few decades, there has been a significant migration of people to urban areas, primarily driven by the availability of better employment opportunities and educational systems. Improved amenities such as transportation, communication, and other services have contributed to the overall livability of cities. The concept of a smart city aims to enhance the quality of life and living standards of people by leveraging the power of the internet and modern technology to address urban challenges. Smart cities rely on sensor data to gain insights into various aspects of city life at different times and locations. Efforts are underway worldwide to establish such well-connected and technologically advanced cities. The utilization of cloud computing, Industry 4.0, and the IoT is integral to the functioning of smart cities. However, the use of these new technologies can lead to potential issues with data, services, and applications in smart cities [24–26].

Each block in the blockchain contains information or a transaction that is time-stamped, making it impossible to alter. This feature ensures that the blockchain is a secure and reliable environment for users. Consensus algorithms that can be implemented on low-power computers are scarce, and mining allows each node to participate in the decision-making process. However, mining requires significant computer power. Existing security and privacy methods are insufficient for intelligent transportation systems. Despite the potential for enhancing efficiency and reducing expenses, blockchain technology faces various challenges and constraints that limit its widespread adoption in numerous industries [27].

It is important to note that blockchain technology should be utilized to replace existing systems that are both time-consuming and costly. DLT has already been employed in communication systems to efficiently manage large amounts of data through separate accounts. Hence, to tackle this problem, a particular blockchain solution is necessary, and that's why a suggestion has been made for a self-governing, interconnected, electric, shared vehicle system without fixed docking points. This system can operate alongside the blockchain platform. In a technologically advanced city, there are various possibilities for implementing transportation systems, like allowing individuals to make payments for transportation through a unified interface while simultaneously accessing shared services. The use of an intelligent transportation system app can also assist individuals and businesses in making informed decisions about where to go and how to navigate the road network efficiently. Additionally, an intelligent transportation system can track micro-mobility in the city and monitor public transportation usage, thereby enhancing the overall efficiency of the transportation system [28].

4.3.7 The Combination of Blockchain and the Internet of Things (IoT) for Banking and Finance

The secure sharing of financial information is made possible by storing it on a distributed ledger. The adoption of blockchain technology in the financial sector is motivated by its decentralized nature, unchangeable records, streamlined processes, cost-efficiency, and enhanced security. It is anticipated that this technology will bring about substantial transformations to the industry within the coming years. Banks must make efforts to decrease the number of individuals engaged in transactions. Banks have allocated greater resources and efforts towards large-scale projects compared to other industries. Given the characteristics of blockchain technology, there is a keen interest in investing in startups that incorporate this technology. Numerous other enterprises are also adopting blockchain technology, and certain individuals have initiated the process of patenting their systems based on blockchain [29]. It is crucial to facilitate banking operations and reduce settlement costs for blockchain companies. Legislators should be trained to make use of these new solutions. It would be more precise to clarify if Bank of America is filing patents for blockchain technology in general or for particular applications. DBS and Standard Chartered Banks are collaborating with Ripple on a trade-finance initiative aimed at optimizing invoice monitoring and preventing redundancy [30], [31]. Financial institutions are interested in investing in and using blockchain technology for several reasons, including:

Decentralization: Blockchain technology allows for a decentralized network, which eliminates the need for a central authority and reduces the chances of fraudulent activities.

Security: Blockchain technology provides a high level of security because it uses advanced cryptographic techniques, making it difficult for hackers to compromise the network.

Efficiency: Blockchain technology enables faster and more efficient transactions by eliminating intermediaries, reducing processing times, and minimizing errors.

Immutability: Once data is recorded on the blockchain, it cannot be altered or deleted, ensuring transparency and accountability.

Cost-effectiveness: Blockchain technology reduces costs by eliminating intermediaries and reducing the need for manual processes, which can lead to significant savings for financial institutions.

4.3.8 The Combination of Blockchain and the Internet of Things (IoT) for Smart Logistics and Customer Relationship Management (CRM)

In Smart Logistics, IoTDs can provide up-to-the-minute information on the location, condition, and status of goods in transit, while blockchain technology can securely record the movement of these goods through the supply chain. This combination can increase transparency, efficiency, and accuracy in logistics management, ultimately leading to reduced costs and greater customer satisfaction [32].

For CRM, blockchain technology can create a transparent and secure record of customer interactions and transactions, while IoTDs can provide valuable data on customer behavior, preferences, and needs. This can enable businesses to offer personalized and targeted marketing, as well as more efficient and effective customer service. Taken together, the integration of blockchain and IoT offers businesses a powerful tool to enhance their logistics and CRM capabilities, resulting in greater efficiency, customer satisfaction, and profitability [33–35].

4.3.9 The Combination of Blockchain and Internet of Things (IoT) for Smart Energy

The use of blockchain and the IoT can bring about a significant transformation in the energy sector through Smart Energy applications. By leveraging IoT sensors and devices, real-time energy usage and production data can be collected and shared across a decentralized blockchain network. This can enhance energy production and usage efficiency, leading to more precise and targeted energy resource management. Moreover, blockchain technology can facilitate secure and transparent energy trading between users on a peer-to-peer basis, bypassing traditional energy providers as intermediaries. This can result in cost savings for consumers and a more decentralized energy market. In summary, the combination of blockchain and IoT has promising implications for the development of Smart Energy systems that can lead to greater sustainability and efficiency in the energy sector [36–40].

4.3.10 The Combination of Blockchain and the Internet of Things (IoT) for Artificial Intelligence (AI)-Based Security

The combination of blockchain and the Internet of Things (IoT) can have a significant impact on artificial intelligence (AI)-based security. By using IoT devices and sensors, real-time data can be collected and analyzed with AI algorithms to identify and respond to security threats. Blockchain technology can provide a secure and transparent record of these security events, enabling the detection and prevention of future threats. The decentralized nature of blockchain technology can also prevent single points of failure, making it harder for attackers to compromise the network, while ensuring data privacy and ownership. Overall, the integration of blockchain, IoT, and AI-based security presents an exciting opportunity to create advanced and secure systems, enhance data privacy, and improve overall cybersecurity [41–55].

Connecting internet-enabled devices, machines, and people in the IoT is a common practice since each device has a unique address that allows it to send data automatically to the web. However, this practice is not safe as IoT applications cannot be kept secure due to their connection to the internet. AI technology has the potential to address the security concerns associated with utilizing blockchain technology, including Bitcoin, Ethereum, and smart contracts, to regulate, oversee, and safeguard IoTDs. By ensuring the confidentiality, integrity, access control, authentication, non-repudiation, and other aspects of data, AI can mitigate the existing security risks involved.

The use of IoT apps has become widespread in various fields, including healthcare, transportation, and weather forecasting. In healthcare, body sensors and physiological data are collected to provide medical attention to disabled people, and it is crucial to maintain the privacy of medical information in these IoT apps [7], [56].

Data integrity in IoT networks pertains to the degree to which data remains intact and unaltered. To ensure secure communication, cryptographic algorithms like Rivest–Shamir–Adleman (RSA), Advanced Encryption Standard (AES), and Triple Data Encryption Standard (TDES) are employed. However, data integrity can be a problem in IoT apps.

Access control measures are crucial to guarantee that only authorized individuals can gain entry to resources within IoT networks. Blockchain technology is used to address this issue, and Bitcoin's quick transfer feature enables efficient access control.

Non-repudiation is a security measure that ensures a device connected to the Internet cannot deny its participation in a transaction. In the realm of IoT applications, techniques such as digital certificates and trust anchors embedded in hardware are employed to guarantee non-repudiation and strengthen security. It is essential to establish strong non-repudiation for users in order to effectively control their access to IoT applications, as merely securing all IoT applications is not enough.

4.4 BLOCKCHAIN FOR INDUSTRY 4.0

The utilization of blockchain technology has the ability to bring about a significant change in Industry 4.0 as it offers a secure and transparent approach for recording, preserving, and exchanging data. By leveraging its DLT, it is possible to establish a decentralized system where transactions and data can be validated and confirmed without the requirement of intermediaries. This, in turn, can improve the management of supply chains, enhance traceability, and decrease instances of fraud and errors. Additionally, the use of smart contracts on the blockchain can automate and simplify processes leading to increased effectiveness and reduced costs. Blockchain technology also creates opportunities for developing new business models and sources of revenue through decentralized marketplaces and tokens. On the whole, blockchain technology has the potential to alter the way businesses function in Industry 4.0 and the future [57].

The industrial history can be categorized into four stages: Industry 1.0 (the Industrial Revolution), Industry 2.0 (the Technological Revolution), Industry 3.0 (the Digital Revolution), and Industry 4.0 (the Fourth Industrial Revolution). These stages were marked by the creation of various technologies that changed the manufacturing industry and resulted in significant societal changes, like the expansion of urban areas and the rise of the service sector. Industry 4.0 aims to establish intelligent factories utilizing digital technologies to enhance efficiency, adaptability, and personalization in response to dynamic market needs.

Smart Solutions: Intelligent products and services have the ability to facilitate novel business models and value propositions.

Smart Products: Innovative ideas can now be created and shared beyond the boundaries of organizations through the development of smart products.

Smart Supply Chains: Digital technologies and cyber-physical systems allow for the creation of supply chains that are both highly integrated and automated.

Smart Factories: Utilizing cyber-physical system integration and decentralized production control allows for a higher degree of self-organization and optimization of processes.

The approach to Industry 4.0 is centered on the use of blockchain technology as a versatile platform that can support multiple industries, including manufacturing, food, pharmaceuticals, healthcare, and creative industries. This is achieved by creating trusted and interconnected networks that eliminate the need for intermediaries. By "distributing trust" among participants, Blockchain allows for the development of new business models in manufacturing. The technology's disruptive potential has already been demonstrated in the financial sector, where it has challenged traditional broker activity by facilitating fast and secure verification of information without human intervention. In addition to financial and professional services, such as property and legal services, Blockchain has the potential to serve as a technology capability platform for all industrial applications.

Healthcare: The implementation of blockchain technology in healthcare can facilitate the creation of a comprehensive medical record for an individual that spans their entire life. Permissioned blockchains can be utilized to ensure confidentiality and privacy by establishing agreements among parties. Through this, authorized parties can access relevant information and transactions as required while safeguarding the privacy of patients and medical professionals.

Education: To combat fraudulent certifications and streamline record-keeping for students and alumni, educational institutions are turning to blockchain technology. The conventional method of using paper-based certification systems is vulnerable to fraud and loss. With the increasing number of people using digital and mobile platforms, a centralized database of credentials and achievements has become necessary.

Government: Governments are investigating the possibility of utilizing blockchain technology to improve their services to the public and streamline administrative processes. The decentralized structure of distributed ledgers presents unique possibilities for governments to enhance transparency, prevent fraudulent activities, and promote confidence among citizens. Through the use of Blockchain to document transactions, governments may discover fresh approaches to attaining these objectives.

Logistics/Transportation: The application of blockchain technology in the logistics, transportation, and supply chain industries has the potential to bring about significant advantages in terms of cost savings and time efficiency. By utilizing blockchain, it is possible to monitor the movement of products and transactions in a new and innovative way, while also providing performance tracking throughout the entire lifecycle of the product. Furthermore, blockchain technology can enable responsible procurement practices that are considerate of environmental and social factors.

4.5 THE COMBINATION OF BLOCKCHAIN AND THE INTERNET OF THINGS (IOT) FOR SOCIETY 5.0

Recent technological advancements, such as the IoT, AI, and robotics, have emerged as influential forces impacting both the economy and society. These developments aim to improve business competitiveness and increase individuals' understanding of their own requirements. The significance of data and these novel technologies, stemming from the Fourth Industrial Revolution, is widely acknowledged by many individuals as a means to tackle societal issues like declining birth rates, aging populations, and environmental and energy-related concerns [57].

Society 5.0 places humans at the center and aims to create a collaborative ecosystem where people, IoTDs, and systems work together. The goal is to leverage IoT data and utilize AI to share it globally. However, the success of Society 5.0 relies on addressing challenges related to data control, misuse, and ownership. Big companies like Google, Apple, Facebook, and Amazon have amassed vast amounts of data, raising concerns about monopolizing and misusing that data. This monopoly hinders small and medium-sized businesses from utilizing data for innovative purposes. In the digital age, it's crucial to share data for the collective benefit while establishing clear protocols for responsible usage and ownership. Blockchain technology provides a transparent ledger where transaction records, ownership details, and commitments can be securely stored. Platforms like Ethereum exemplify blockchain's capabilities by enabling the creation of digital smart contracts, facilitating the execution of significant legal actions based on predefined agreements. Unlike centralized data monopolies, public blockchain data is accessible to all, ensuring a more open and inclusive approach.

4.6 CONCLUSION

The revolutionary blockchain technology has garnered considerable attention from researchers and businesses alike. However, the extensive media coverage surrounding blockchain can make it challenging to make an unbiased investment decision in this field. Businesses are taking a risk by adopting blockchain, not because they believe it is fully ready for implementation in society and companies, but rather out of curiosity. Nevertheless, progress has been made in developing new architectures that enhance security and data transparency. In the context of smart agriculture, blockchain-based solutions utilize unified smart home resource services, where users need to verify their identities through smart contracts. This approach enables faster and safer utilization of services while eliminating the need for repetitive authentication. Intelligent cities aim to enhance the quality of life for residents through innovative and advanced services. However, it is crucial to recognize that diverse methods of collecting, storing, processing, and analyzing data can create vulnerabilities. Factors such as the Internet of Things (IoT), cloud computing, and social media could potentially lead to unauthorized access to smart city data and applications in the future. This vulnerability poses a risk to the security of sensitive information, emphasizing the need for resolution. Blockchain technology is increasingly being employed across various sectors, including IoT, healthcare, and finance, giving rise to new markets. Companies are leveraging this technology to gain a competitive edge and address their present and future needs.

REFERENCES

[1] K. Pal, "Internet of things and blockchain technology in apparel manufacturing supply chain data management," *Procedia Computer Science*, vol. 170, pp. 450–457, 2020.

[2] M. Vivekanandan, S. VN, and S. R. U, "BIDAPSCA5G: Blockchain based Internet of Things (IoT) device to device authentication protocol for smart city applications using 5G technology," *Peer-to-Peer networking and applications*, vol. 14, pp. 403–419, 2021.

[3] A. D. Dwivedi, L. Malina, P. Dzurenda, and G. Srivastava, "Optimized blockchain model for internet of things based healthcare applications," in *2019 42nd international conference on telecommunications and signal processing (TSP)*, IEEE, 2019, pp. 135–139.

[4] A. Dhar Dwivedi, R. Singh, K. Kaushik, R. Rao Mukkamala, and W. S. Alnumay, "Blockchain and artificial intelligence for 5G-enabled Internet of Things: Challenges, opportunities, and solutions," *Transactions on Emerging Telecommunications Technologies*, p. e4329, 2021.

[5] N. Hossein Motlagh, M. Mohammadrezaei, J. Hunt, and B. Zakeri, "Internet of Things (IoT) and the energy sector," *Energies*, vol. 13, no. 2, p. 494, 2020.

[6] N. S. Alghamdi and M. A. Khan, "Energy-Efficient and Blockchain-Enabled Model for Internet of Things (IoT) in Smart Cities.," *Computers, Materials & Continua*, vol. 66, no. 3, pp. 2509–2524, 2021.

[7] R. Chaganti, V. Varadarajan, V. S. Gorantla, T. R. Gadekallu, and V. Ravi, "Blockchain-based cloud-enabled security monitoring using internet of things in smart agriculture," *Future Internet*, vol. 14, no. 9, p. 250, 2022.

[8] M. R. Bataineh, W. Mardini, Y. M. Khamayseh, and M. M. B. Yassein, "Novel and Secure Blockchain Framework for Health Applications in IoT," *IEEE Access*, vol. 10, pp. 14914–14926, 2022, doi: 10.1109/ACCESS.2022.3147795.

[9] A. H. Sodhro, S. Pirbhulal, M. Muzammal, and L. Zongwei, "Towards blockchain-enabled security technique for industrial internet of things based decentralized applications," *Journal of Grid Computing*, vol. 18, pp. 615–628, 2020.

[10] R. Singh, A. D. Dwivedi, and G. Srivastava, "Internet of things based blockchain for temperature monitoring and counterfeit pharmaceutical prevention," *Sensors*, vol. 20, no. 14, p. 3951, 2020.

[11] M. A. F. Noor, S. Khanum, T. Anwar, and M. Ansari, "A Holistic View on Blockchain and Its Issues," in *Blockchain Applications in IoT Security*, IGI Global, 2021, pp. 21–44.

[12] W. Chen, S. M. Bohloul, Y. Ma, and L. Li, "A blockchain-based information management system for academic institutions: a case study of international students' workflow," *Information Discovery and Delivery*, vol. 50, no. 4, pp. 343–352, 2022.

[13] M. Mohy-eddine, A. Guezzaz, S. Benkirane, and M. Azrour, "IoT-Enabled Smart Agriculture: Security Issues and Applications," in *Artificial Intelligence and Smart Environment: ICAISE'2022*, Springer, 2023, pp. 566–571.

[14] J. Mabrouki *et al.*, "Smart system for monitoring and controlling of agricultural production by the IoT," in *IoT and Smart Devices for Sustainable Environment*, Springer, 2022, pp. 103–115.

[15] M. K. Boutahir, Y. Farhaoui, M. Azrour, I. Zeroual, and A. El Allaoui, "Effect of Feature Selection on the Prediction of Direct Normal Irradiance," *Big Data Mining and Analytics*, vol. 5, no. 4, pp. 309–317, Dec. 2022, doi: 10.26599/ BDMA.2022.9020003.

[16] H. Hissou, S. Benkirane, A. Guezzaz, M. Azrour, and A. Beni-Hssane, "A Novel Machine Learning Approach for Solar Radiation Estimation," *Sustainability*, vol. 15, no. 13, Art. no. 13, Jan. 2023, doi: 10.3390/su151310609.

[17] M. K. Boutahir, Y. Farhaoui, and M. Azrour, "Machine Learning and Deep Learning Applications for Solar Radiation Predictions Review: Morocco as a Case of Study," in *Digital Economy, Business Analytics, and Big Data Analytics Applications*, Springer, 2022, pp. 55–67.

[18] J. Sedlmeir, H. U. Buhl, G. Fridgen, and R. Keller, "The energy consumption of blockchain technology: Beyond myth," *Business & Information Systems Engineering*, vol. 62, no. 6, pp. 599–608, 2020.

[19] S. Dhiviya, S. Malathy, and D. R. Kumar, "Internet of things (IoT) elements, trends and applications," *Journal of computational and theoretical nanoscience*, vol. 15, no. 5, pp. 1639–1643, 2018.

[20] I. Tibrewal, M. Srivastava, and A. K. Tyagi, "Blockchain technology for securing cyber-infrastructure and internet of things networks," *Intelligent Interactive Multimedia Systems for e-Healthcare Applications*, pp. 337–350, 2022.

[21] W. Ejaz, A. Anpalagan, W. Ejaz, and A. Anpalagan, "Blockchain technology for security and privacy in internet of things," *Internet of Things for Smart Cities: Technologies, Big Data and Security*, pp. 47–55, 2019.

[22] A. Tchagna Kouanou *et al.*, "Securing data in an internet of things network using blockchain technology: smart home case," *SN Computer Science*, vol. 3, no. 2, p. 167, 2022.

[23] Q. Song, Y. Chen, Y. Zhong, K. Lan, S. Fong, and R. Tang, "A supply-chain system framework based on internet of things using blockchain technology," *ACM Transactions on Internet Technology (TOIT)*, vol. 21, no. 1, pp. 1–24, 2021.

[24] P. Manjunath, R. Soman, and P. G. Shah, "IoT and block chain driven intelligent transportation system," in *2018 Second International Conference on Green Computing and Internet of Things (ICGCIoT)*, IEEE, 2018, pp. 290–293.

[25] J. Chen, S. Xu, K. Liu, S. Yao, X. Luo, and H. Wu, "Intelligent Transportation Logistics Optimal Warehouse Location Method Based on Internet of Things and Blockchain Technology," *Sensors*, vol. 22, no. 4, p. 1544, 2022.

[26] M. B. Mollah *et al.*, "Blockchain for the internet of vehicles towards intelligent transportation systems: A survey," *IEEE Internet of Things Journal*, vol. 8, no. 6, pp. 4157–4185, 2020.

[27] M. Kamran, H. U. Khan, W. Nisar, M. Farooq, and S.-U. Rehman, "Blockchain and Internet of Things: A bibliometric study," *Computers & Electrical Engineering*, vol. 81, p. 106525, 2020.

[28] M. Humayun, N. Z. Jhanjhi, B. Hamid, and G. Ahmed, "Emerging smart logistics and transportation using IoT and blockchain," *IEEE Internet of Things Magazine*, vol. 3, no. 2, pp. 58–62, 2020.

[29] S. Singh and N. Singh, "Blockchain: Future of financial and cyber security," in *2016 2nd International Conference on Contemporary Computing and Informatics (IC3I)*, Dec. 2016, pp. 463–467. doi: 10.1109/IC3I.2016.7918009.

[30] L. Liu, J. Z. Zhang, W. He, and W. Li, "Mitigating information asymmetry in inventory pledge financing through the Internet of things and blockchain," *Journal of Enterprise Information Management*, vol. 34, no. 5, pp. 1429–1451, 2021.

[31] Y. Zhang and J. Wen, "The IoT electric business model: Using blockchain technology for the internet of things," *Peer-to-Peer Netw. Appl.*, vol. 10, no. 4, pp. 983–994, Jul. 2017, doi: 10.1007/s12083-016-0456-1.

[32] J. Chen, S. Xu, K. Liu, S. Yao, X. Luo, and H. Wu, "Intelligent Transportation Logistics Optimal Warehouse Location Method Based on Internet of Things and Blockchain Technology," *Sensors*, vol. 22, no. 4, p. 1544, 2022.

[33] Y. Issaoui, A. Khiat, A. Bahnasse, and H. Ouajji, "Smart logistics: Study of the application of blockchain technology," *Procedia Computer Science*, vol. 160, pp. 266–271, 2019.

[34] D. D. Sivaganesan, "Block chain enabled internet of things," *Journal of Information Technology and Digital World*, vol. 1, no. 1, pp. 1–8, 2019.

[35] Y. Song, F. R. Yu, L. Zhou, X. Yang, and Z. He, "Applications of the Internet of Things (IoT) in smart logistics: A comprehensive survey," *IEEE Internet of Things Journal*, vol. 8, no. 6, pp. 4250–4274, 2020.

[36] J. Mabrouki *et al.*, "Smart system for monitoring and controlling of agricultural production by the IoT," in *IoT and Smart Devices for Sustainable Environment*, Springer, 2022, pp. 103–115.

[37] J. Mabrouki, M. Azrour, G. Fattah, D. Dhiba, and S. El Hajjaji, "Intelligent monitoring system for biogas detection based on the Internet of Things: Mohammedia, Morocco city landfill case," *Big Data Mining and Analytics*, vol. 4, no. 1, pp. 10–17, 2021.

[38] N. Renugadevi, S. Saravanan, and C. N. Sudha, "IoT based smart energy grid for sustainable cites," *Materials Today: Proceedings*, vol. 81, part 2, pp. 98–104, 2023.

[39] N. S. Alghamdi and M. A. Khan, "Energy-Efficient and Blockchain-Enabled Model for Internet of Things (IoT) in Smart Cities," *Computers, Materials & Continua*, vol. 66, no. 3, pp. 2509–2524, 2021.

[40] J. Mabrouki, M. Azrour, and S. E. Hajjaji, "Use of internet of things for monitoring and evaluating water's quality: a comparative study," *International Journal of Cloud Computing*, vol. 10, no. 5–6, pp. 633–644, 2021.

[41] L. Nforh CheSuh, R. Á. Fernández Díaz, J. M. Alija Perez, C. Benavides Cuellar, and H. Alaiz Moretón, "Improve Quality of Service for the Internet of Things Using Blockchain & Machine Learning Algorithms," *Ramón Ángel and Alija Perez, Jose Manuel and Benavides Cuellar, Cármen and Alaiz Moretón, Héctor, Improve Quality of Service for the Internet of Things Using Blockchain & Machine Learning Algorithms*.

[42] S. Shaw, Z. Rowland, and V. Machova, "Internet of Things smart devices, sustainable industrial big data, and artificial intelligence-based decision-making algorithms in cyber-physical system-based manufacturing," *Economics, Management and Financial Markets*, vol. 16, no. 2, pp. 106–116, 2021.

[43] R. L. Kumar, Y. Wang, T. Poongodi, and A. L. Imoize, *Internet of Things, artificial intelligence and blockchain technology*. Springer, 2021.

[44] S. Amaouche *et al.*, "FSCB-IDS: Feature Selection and Minority Class Balancing for Attacks Detection in VANETS," *Applied sciences*, vol. 13, no. 13, p. 7488, 2023.

[45] S. Khan *et al.*, "Manufacturing industry based on dynamic soft sensors in integrated with feature representation and classification using fuzzy logic and deep learning architecture," *Int J Adv Manuf Technol*, Jun. 2023, doi: 10.1007/s00170-023-11602-y.

[46] M. Azrour, M. Ouanan, Y. Farhaoui, and A. Guezzaz, "Security analysis of Ye et al. authentication protocol for Internet of Things," in *Big Data and Smart Digital Environment*, Springer, 2019, pp. 67–74.

[47] S. Dargaoui *et al.*, "An Overview of the Security Challenges in IoT Environment," in *Advanced Technology for Smart Environment and Energy*, J. Mabrouki, A. Mourade, A. Irshad, and S. A. Chaudhry, Eds., in Environmental Science and Engineering. Cham: Springer International Publishing, 2023, pp. 151–160. doi: 10.1007/978-3-031-25662-2_13.

[48] M. Mohy-Eddine, M. Azrour, J. Mabrouki, F. Amounas, A. Guezzaz, and S. Benkirane, "Embedded Web Server Implementation for Real-Time Water Monitoring," in *Advanced Technology for Smart Environment and Energy*, J. Mabrouki, A. Mourade, A. Irshad, and S. A. Chaudhry, Eds., in Environmental Science and Engineering. Cham: Springer International Publishing, 2023, pp. 301–311. doi: 10.1007/978-3-031-25662-2_24.

[49] C. Hazman, S. Benkirane, A. Guezzaz, M. Azrour, and M. Abdedaime, "Building an Intelligent Anomaly Detection Model with Ensemble Learning for IoT-Based Smart Cities," in *Advanced Technology for Smart Environment and Energy*, Springer, 2023, pp. 287–299.

[50] H. Attou, A. Guezzaz, S. Benkirane, M. Azrour, and Y. Farhaoui, "Cloud-Based Intrusion Detection Approach Using Machine Learning Techniques," *Big Data Mining and Analytics*, vol. 6, no. 3, pp. 311–320, 2023.

[51] M. Mohy-eddine, A. Guezzaz, S. Benkirane, and M. Azrour, "An effective intrusion detection approach based on ensemble learning for IIoT edge computing," *Journal of Computer Virology and Hacking Techniques*, pp. 1–13, 2022.

[52] M. Mohy-eddine, A. Guezzaz, S. Benkirane, and M. Azrour, "An efficient network intrusion detection model for IoT security using K-NN classifier and feature selection," *Multimedia Tools and Applications*, 2023, doi: 10.1007/s11042-023-14795-2.

[53] M. Mohy-eddine, S. Benkirane, A. Guezzaz, and M. Azrour, "Random forest-based IDS for IIoT edge computing security using ensemble learning for dimensionality reduction," vol. 15, no. 6, pp. 467–474.

[54] M. Douiba, S. Benkirane, A. Guezzaz, and M. Azrour, "Anomaly detection model based on gradient boosting and decision tree for IoT environments security," *Journal of Reliable Intelligent Environments*, pp. 1–12, 2022.

[55] M. Douiba, S. Benkirane, A. Guezzaz, and M. Azrour, "An improved anomaly detection model for IoT security using decision tree and gradient boosting," *The Journal of Supercomputing*, vol. 79, no. 3, pp. 3392–3411, 2022.

[56] I. Abu-Elezz, A. Hassan, A. Nazeemudeen, M. Househ, and A. Abd-Alrazaq, "The benefits and threats of blockchain technology in healthcare: A scoping review," *International Journal of Medical Informatics*, vol. 142, p. 104246, 2020.

[57] A. K. Tyagi, S. Dananjayan, D. Agarwal, and H. F. Thariq Ahmed, "Blockchain—Internet of Things Applications: Opportunities and Challenges for Industry 4.0 and Society 5.0," *Sensors*, vol. 23, no. 2, Art. no. 2, Jan. 2023, doi: 10.3390/s23020947.

CHAPTER 5

Security Issues in Internet of Medical Things

Souhayla Dargaoui, Mourade Azrour, Jamal Mabrouki, Ahmad El Allaoui, Azidine Guezzaz, Said Benkirane, and Abdulatif Alabdulatif

5.1 INTRODUCTION

The concept of the Internet of Things (IoT) refers to a set of devices that have various abilities, like the sensing and collecting of data, processing and analyzing collected data, and communicating with each other via the internet or other communication networks [1]–[11]. Furthermore, the IoT's central intention is to be adept at setting up, controlling, and interconnecting, at the same time, devices or objects that are typically never connected to the internet, for example, thermometers, fridges, TVs, irrigation pumps, vehicles, electric meters, agriculture smarter, medical devices, and so on. Hence, IoT is deployed in various domains [12]–[15].

Recently, the COVID-19 outbreak has further accentuated the necessity of developing smart health systems that provide prevention, remote diagnosis, and treatment [16]. The new advanced health services are not merely a refinement of technology; in fact, they are a universal and multilevel

DOI: 10.1201/9781003438779-5

revolution in the health sector. Such services are founded on emerging new technology, including the cloud, the IoT, deep learning, machine learning, blockchain, and big data [17]–[22].

In healthcare applications, the IoT is known as the Internet of Medical Things (IoMT). Hence, it involves medical devices which are connected to patients in order to detect medical parameters. That information is then shared with healthcare operators [23], [24]. Thanks to the IoMT, many medical devices and applications can communicate via the internet, and this development has altered healthcare notions in recent years. Across the medical sector, wearable IoT devices (IoTDs) have helped to lead the way into the era of smart health services. Accordingly, they have supported patient health monitoring in a safe manner as well as enhancing existing hospital infrastructures.

However, the deployment of the IoMT has revealed various challenges and issues such as medical device heterogeneity, the complexity of medical applications, device storage and processor performance, network resource limitations, real-time data processing, low-power devices, security, and data confidentiality. Besides, authentication is a prime security service that must be assured in any medical system. Hence, in this paper, we review the security and privacy solutions, especially the authentication methods that are used for IoT-based healthcare systems.

The remainder of this paper is organized as follows. Section 5.2 presents related works. In Section 5.3, we give some details about background information. Section 5.4 discusses the security exigencies in smart healthcare systems. In Section 5.5, we present an authentication protocol classification. Finally, Section 5.6 concludes the paper.

5.2 RELATED WORKS

Over the last few years, IoMT-based healthcare solutions have received much attention from many researchers. Considering the large personal data flows generated by such networks, data security becomes a key challenge ahead of their deployment. In this regard, several authentication and key accord protocols have been suggested to guarantee confidentiality and security in IoMT environments. Maria Papaioannou et al. presented a "Survey on Security Threats and Countermeasures in the Internet of Medical Things" [25]. The paper presents at first a classification of confidentiality threats to edge networks in terms of the security service targeted; secondly, it provides a classification of security measures for attacks that occur in the IoMT edge network environment. Mudassar Mushtaq et al. published a paper with the purpose of introducing some threats that target IoMT environments [26]. R. Somasundaram et al. [27] provided a review that summarizes all confidentiality challenges related to the IoMT and several countermeasures for these issues. The paper analyzes many issues to identify several risk factors. The experimental results prove that Distributed Denial of Services is the most dangerous attack in IoMT networks. Amsaveni Avainashiappan et al. [28] provided a chapter that presents an overview of security attacks and issues in the IoMT, then they provide several proven solutions which can be implemented to improve confidentiality in such environments. Neha Garg et al. [29] provided a comprehensive review of security challenges in IoMT-based smart healthcare. At first, they present several IoMT communication architectures. Additionally, they highlight IoMT confidentiality requirements and provide an adversary model of IoMT communication. They also suggest a simple taxonomy of security schemes and provide a detailed comparison study between several protocols in terms of various parameters, such as computational cost, communication cost, and security services.

5.3 BACKGROUND

5.3.1 Healthcare 4.0

The German manufacturing industries consolidated the competitiveness of their sector in 2011 by supporting a new concept, thanks to the participation of innovators from different fields such as medicine, academia, and industries. The concept was named "Industry 4.0" at the first edition of the Hannover Trade Fair. The German government has been very supportive of this concept, considering that Industry 4.0 will develop in the coming years [30]. Hence, Industry 4.0 has established a new model for the manufacturing industry (Figure 5.1). Since then, emerging technologies such as data digitizing, data visualizing, business intelligence, and machine learning are booming. A similar situation has happened in the healthcare industry as well, particularly as it is now on the verge of a foundational change in the new age with the emergent usage of intelligent and interconnected healthcare-related devices [31].

In addition, Healthcare 4.0 identifies several key challenges and opportunities in applying robotics together with automated, novel processes to revolutionize the current pharmaceutical systems, the IoT, and embedded daily networks to empower and reinforce data for generating enhanced healthcare implications for people [32].

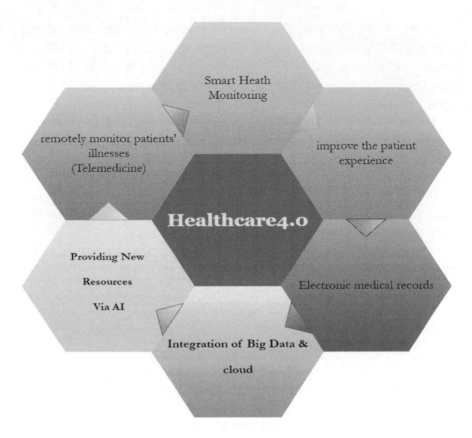

FIGURE 5.1 Healthcare capabilities

5.3.2 IoT-Based Healthcare

Recently, the usage of IoT design, especially when it is implemented in the manufacturing sector, is largely called IoT 4.0. It can actually be viewed as moving past the IoT, whether that means the addition of baseline infrastructures in conjunction with the specifics of manufacturing and other logistics, or alternatively, it means the inclusion overlay of IoT capabilities on existing automated processes, with some new opportunities as a consequence [33]. Certainly, healthcare has emerged as being among the most attractive domains for applying the IoT [34]. The successful implementation of such an ecosystem model is remodeling the concept of healthcare, showing great technological, business, and life opportunities. Therefore, the IoT is probably the main enabler of distributed healthcare applications [35], [36], significantly helping to decrease the aggregate cost of healthcare as well as increasing health outputs, although behavioral changes to the system stakeholders are needed. Besides, the advancements in Wireless Sensor Network (WSN) and the associated enhancements in terms of performance significantly promote real-time monitoring of human physiological metrics. Consequently, IoMT facilitates chronic illness treatments, allowing earlier diagnoses and managment of medical emergency situations [23], [37–39]. In these terms, embedded devices, wearable devices, and imaging devices are essential to facilitate the deployment of the IoT in healthcare. Nevertheless, despite the great advancement of IoT applications in healthcare systems, many challenges and issues are waiting for novel solutions. Accordingly, in Section 5.2.2, we discuss some challenges and issues that appear after the deployment of the IoT in healthcare.

5.3.3 Challenges and Issues

5.3.3.1 Interoperability and Standardization Protocols

Indeed, there are many standards which can be used to implement various applications developed by the different industries. More than that, the interchange of a variety of datasets results in a large dataset in the IoMT environment. This diversity among the various devices and acquired data from multiple sources restricts the scale of usage, which is driven principally by interoperability between the operators. Hence, interoperability is a challenge because the exchange and sharing of data between various IoMT systems that have dissimilar specifications becomes problematic. As a result, the ensuing standards for such systems become important, particularly in those applications that allow for interorganizational cross-platform systems.

5.3.3.2 Privacy and Security

One of the major difficulties and challenges in implementing the IoMT is to ensure an adequate cybersecurity system. Hence, maintaining the confidentiality and privacy associated with the overwhelming volume of personal health data shared between devices is always an ongoing challenge. Usually, healthcare, and its related data security in an IoMT cloud-based healthcare environment, is provided by using a deterministic algorithm and a symmetric key that encrypts data in blocks. Recently, blockchain technology has been used to address security and privacy concerns, as well as to prevent the introduction of personal information while increasing storage capacity. Table 5.1 illustrates some security threats.

TABLE 5.1   Security threats

Attacks Type	Description	Target Layer	Example of Attacks
Active attacks	This type of attack is mainly designed to perform harmful activities against the operating system, causing damage or disturbance to the legitimate users' services. These attacks violate both the system's confidentiality and integrity.	Network	DoS, DDoS, Man-in-the-Middle
Active attacks	Attacks when an opponent attempts to deny or repudiate the actions that they have taken. In other words, it refers to the capability of communicating parties to deny the authenticity of their signature on any document or the transmission of a message that they initiated.	Application	Message, transaction repudiation attacks
Passive attacks	This type of attack doesn't have any influence on the system resources and can't change data, however, it's dangerous for confidentiality and privacy. Its main object is to observe communicated messages and save them for malicious purposes.	Network	Sniffing

5.4 INTRODUCTION DATA SECURITY REQUIREMENTS IN SMART HEALTHCARE SYSTEMS

Cybersecurity goals in smart healthcare systems necessitate the usage of precautions to deliver information security 17]. It is imperative that such key security principles be addressed in IoMT-based solutions. In addition to discussing the different security threats practiced and applied by hackers, in the below section, we will mention some of the related security requirements for smart healthcare systems. Thus, the goal of this section is to present several security exigencies for a smart healthcare system. As demonstrated in Figure 5.2, there are basic security services expected in IoMT smart solutions, such as authorization, authentication, confidentiality, availability, integrity, and non-repudiation.

FIGURE 5.2   Security services required for smart healthcare

Non-repudiation: This is the assurance that someone cannot deny anything. Generally, non-repudiation refers to the ability to guarantee that a party to a contract or communication cannot deny the authenticity of their signature on a document or the sending of a message that they originated.

Availability: A key availability requirement is to ensure that networks are always working. In more detail, the availability of transmission bandwidth and the necessary service or data should be guaranteed by a security infrastructure at any moment. In the case of infrastructure, encryption and trusted devices allow the security of the networks. Additionally, in situations that are completely distributed, the trust-based approach standing by itself can provide a preferred alternative to cryptographically based approaches.

Authentication: This is the procedure that permits the verification of the system user's identity. Therefore, it is vital to make sure that the data comes from a reliable source. If the authenticity of the data is not guaranteed, attackers may retrieve data exchanged in an IoT network, or usurp fake data in the system, pretending to be from legitimate and reliable sources.

Integrity: This is one of the most important information security requirements, which ensures protection against any illegitimate modification of the data, whether voluntary or accidental, during transmission, processing, or storage. Ensuring integrity is essential to ensure that the information provided by the source is the information received by the destination or destinations.

Confidentiality: This security service ensures that only authorized entities can access data resources. In IoT systems and especially in communication, cryptographic mechanisms are used to guarantee the confidentiality of data.

5.5 AUTHENTICATION PROTOCOLS CLASSIFICATION

Security issues include weak login and password security. Several IoT systems currently use password security to prevent hackers from trying to obtain unauthorized access. Such passwords in many instances are potentially very weak, so criminals could easily have remote access to an IoT unit. Currently, no standards have been set regarding the sophistication and complexity required for passwords [40–42]. Nonetheless, recent studies demonstrate that using more complex passwords combined with other factors in IoT systems could prevent even more attacks. Generally, the authentication procedure in IoMT structures might depend on four different schemes including basic, key-based, certificate-based, or cryptography-based. However, scientists have newly approved crossbreed patterns to enhance the security capabilities of IoMT systems.

In the case of simple authentication, the factors that identify an object or user are used for performing the authentication process of this object or user. Hence, the manners in which the factors are used determine the effectiveness of each authentication scheme. Even if only two factors are used in the situation of basic authentication, many protocols are subject to three factors by joining knowledge, inheritance, and possession credentials.

With the recent use of the IoT in the field of healthcare, a lot of patient data is being transmitted and made available online. This necessitates sufficient security measures to be put in place to prevent the possibility of cyberattacks. In this regard, several authentication techniques have been proposed recently to mitigate these challenges, but the physical security of healthcare IoTDs against node tampering and node replacement attacks is not addressed sufficiently in the literature. Therefore, in this section, we discuss authentication protocols that have been proposed in the literature.

5.5.1 ECC-based

Based on elliptic curve cryptography (ECC), Xu et al. [20] proposed a mutual authentication and key convention scheme as a solution to the computational problem. Then, they demonstrated that the proposed protocol guarantees confidentiality by using a dynamic identity. Furthermore, Yan et al. [21] proposed a user authentication system based on biometric detection. However, this protocol cannot resist replay attacks and is not able to guarantee user anonymity. Furthermore, Mishra et al. proved that Yan's protocol is vulnerable to offline password guessing attacks. Based on those issues, Mishra et al. [22] suggested a new reinforced biometric authentication protocol that uses random digits. Afterward, Tan [23] proposed a three-factor mutual authentication protocol.

In 2012, He et al. [25] proposed an authentication protocol which is efficient for actual medical applications that are based on a sensor network. Nevertheless, the scheme is prone to forgery attacks and password guessing attacks. In addition, it is not capable of offering forward privacy service. In 2014, Mishra et al. [26] relied on chaotic map computation for presenting an authentication and key exchanging protocol for healthcare information organisms. However, this scheme is vulnerable to password guessing attacks

5.5.2 Blockchain-Based

A healthcare-oriented blockchain protocol was proposed by Zhao et al. [43] in 2018. Within this protocol and, in order to protect the relevant patient records, the blockchain is employed to secure the patient's data. Even though the blockchain is viewed as a very public network, the possibility that attackers may be able to have access to sensitive details is present. However, in this case, the actual data is saved in a public address, so it is not easy for an attacker to compromise this data. Furthermore, the scheme is appropriate when storing a high volume of content. Nevertheless, there is no proper authentication process for transferring patients' confidential details between doctors, and therefore, the processing time becomes more expensive and time-consuming. As a result, the computational complexity increases in this scheme.

In 2022, Rajasekaran and Azees [44] proposed a mutual authentication for smart healthcare based on blockchain. Initially, in this proposed protocol, the authentication is accomplished between all end-users. Hence, it is followed by encryption/decryption of personal transmitted information. Moreover, in order to eliminate the re-authentication of patients during the movement of a patient from doctor to doctor, a handshake authentication procedure is executed between the doctors, which enhances the analysis of the performances. In the section on security analysis, the authors demonstrated the resistance of their proposed scheme against different susceptible attacks.

The authors of [45] proposed a dual centralized and distributed hybrid authentication architecture using blockchain and Edge computing-based technologies. This protocol addresses efficiently the scale-up challenges related to heterogeneous IoT networks, such as the possibility to connect seamlessly a high number of trustworthy IoT nodes from various IoT systems.

5.5.3 Smart Card-Based

There are many symmetrical keying approaches which have been suggested in the published literature regarding smart card authentication in both single-server and multi-server environments. In addition to smart card authentication, three-factor authentication approaches that rely on biometric credentials are discussed in the literature. However, the incorporation of biometric data is tied to a static string and performed in a similar way to entering a password. Such smart card-enabled processes can be readily translated into a biometric shape and the other way around. The majority of authentication methods based on smart cards and provided biometrics are not safe for well-known attacks like smart card steal attacks, replay attacks, impersonation attacks, and insider attacks [46].

5.5.4 Signature-Based

In [47], an approach to better secure and enhance the quality of the e-healthcare system in the COVID-19 scenario is addressed. A multifactor authentication scheme using round-band signatures is evaluated to ensure a high-quality IoMT system. The cryptosystem of KMOV ensures confidentiality in the suggested scheme. In the proposed protocol, the security evaluation model establishes that the asset is highly secured. Both the formal and informal security analyses demonstrate that the proposed scheme is resistant to all possible attacks.

5.5.5 Hash Function-Based

Recently, Abdussami et al. [48] presented a lightweight authentication and key establishment protocol that is necessary for patient monitoring and diagnostics systems. It ensures the anonymity of both patients and doctors and also facilitates the task of patients' family members with periodic status updates. Formal evaluation using the real-or-random (ROR) model demonstrates that this protocol is semantically secure. Furthermore, both the simulation findings and the informal analyses prove that the suggested scheme overcomes the various potential attacks.

5.6 CONCLUSION

IoMT technology is the most widely used and discussed technology in recent smart healthcare systems research. It is a matter of improving the patient experience, based on various technologies and devices, that are different in terms of energy, computing power, and storage memory. This heterogeneity in technologies and standards and device limitation leads to security issues that extend across all IoMT architecture layers. As a result, security is always looking for ways to improve network reliability and protect from attacks. Authentication is the entrance gate that can be used by user or device when they want to have an access to a network. It is one of the most important parts in IoMT security. In this paper we presented some challenges and threats to IoMT security, then we provided some data security requirements in smart healthcare systems, and at the end, we offered a simple classification of the existing authentication methods which resist well-known attacks.

REFERENCES

1. S. Khan, A. S. Al-Mogren, and M. F. AlAjmi, "Using cloud computing to improve network operations and management," in *2015 5th National Symposium on Information Technology: Towards New Smart World (NSITNSW)*, IEEE, 2015, pp. 1–6.
2. J. Khan et al., "Secure smart healthcare monitoring in industrial Internet of Things (IIoT) ecosystem with cosine function hybrid chaotic map encryption," *Scientific Programming*, vol. 2022, 2022.
3. S. Ahmad et al., "Deep learning enabled disease diagnosis for secure internet of medical things." Computers, Materials & Continua, vol. 73, no 1, 2022, pp. 965–979.
4. A. Guezzaz, S. Benkirane, and M. Azrour, "A novel anomaly network intrusion detection system for Internet of Things security," in *IoT and Smart Devices for Sustainable Environment*, Springer, 2022, pp. 129–138.
5. J. Mabrouki et al., "Smart system for monitoring and controlling of agricultural production by the IoT," in *IoT and Smart Devices for Sustainable Environment*, Springer, 2022, pp. 103–115.
6. A. Guezzaz, M. Azrour, S. Benkirane, M. Mohyeddine, H. Attou, and M. Douiba, "A lightweight hybrid intrusion detection framework using machine learning for edge-based IIoT security," *International Arab Journal of Information Technology*, vol. 19, no. 5, 2022, pp. 822–830
7. G. Fattah, J. Mabrouki, F. Ghrissi, M. Azrour, and Y. Abrouki, "Multi-sensor system and Internet of Things (IoT) technologies for air pollution monitoring," in *Futuristic Research Trends and Applications of Internet of Things*, CRC Press, 2022.

8. M. Douiba, S. Benkirane, A. Guezzaz, and M. Azrour, "Anomaly detection model based on gradient boosting and decision tree for IoT environments security," *Journal of Reliable Intelligent Environments*, pp. 1–12, 2022.

9. M. Douiba, S. Benkirane, A. Guezzaz, and M. Azrour, "An improved anomaly detection model for IoT security using decision tree and gradient boosting," *The Journal of Supercomputing*, pp. 1–20, 2022.

10. M. Mohy-eddine, A. Guezzaz, S. Benkirane, and M. Azrour, "An effective intrusion detection approach based on ensemble learning for IIoT edge computing," *Journal of Computer Virology and Hacking Techniques*, pp. 1–13, 2022.

11. C. Hazman, A. Guezzaz, S. Benkirane, and M. Azrour, "LIDS-SIoEL: Intrusion detection framework for IoT-based smart environments security using ensemble learning," *Cluster Computing*, pp. 1–15, 2022.

12. S. Benkirane et al., "Adapted speed system in a road bend situation in VANET environment," *Computers, Materials & Continua*, vol. 74, no. 2, pp. 3781–3794, 2023, doi: 10.32604/cmc.2023.033119.

13. J. Mabrouki, M. Azrour, and S. E. Hajjaji, "Use of internet of things for monitoring and evaluating water's quality: A comparative study," *International Journal of Cloud Computing*, vol. 10, no. 5–6, pp. 633–644, 2021.

14. M. Azrour, M. Ouanan, Y. Farhaoui, and A. Guezzaz, "Security analysis of Ye et al. Authentication protocol for Internet of Things," in *Big Data and Smart Digital Environment*, Y. Farhaoui and L. Moussaid, Eds. Springer International Publishing, 2019, pp. 67–74. doi: 10.1007/978-3-030-12 048-1_9.

15. M. Azrour, Y. Farhaoui, M. Ouanan, and A. Guezzaz, "SPIT detection in telephony over IP using K-Means algorithm," *Procedia Computer Science*, vol. 148, pp. 542–551, 2019, doi: 10.1016/j.procs.2019.01.027.

16. R. Praveen and P. Pabitha, "Improved Gentry–Halevi's fully homomorphic encryption-based lightweight privacy preserving scheme for securing medical Internet of Things," *Transactions on Emerging Telecommunications Technologies*, vol. n/a, no. n/a, p. e4732, doi: 10.1002/ett.4732.

17. M. K. Boutahir, Y. Farhaoui, and M. Azrour, "Machine learning and deep learning applications for solar radiation predictions review: Morocco as a case of study," in *Digital Economy, Business Analytics, and Big Data Analytics Applications*, S. G. Yaseen, Ed., in Studies in Computational Intelligence, vol. 1010. Cham: Springer International Publishing, 2022, pp. 55–67. doi: 10.1007/978-3-031-05258-3_6.

18. R. Chaganti, A. Mourade, V. Ravi, N. Vemprala, A. Dua, and B. Bhushan, "A particle swarm optimization and deep learning approach for intrusion detection system in internet of medical things," *Sustainability*, vol. 14, no. 19, p. 12828, Oct. 2022, doi: 10.3390/su141912828.

19. A. Guezzaz, Y. Asimi, M. Azrour, and A. Asimi, "Mathematical validation of proposed machine learning classifier for heterogeneous traffic and anomaly detection," *Big Data Mining and Analytics*, vol. 4, no. 1, pp. 18–24, Mar. 2021, doi: 10.26599/BDMA.2020.9020019.

20. M. Azrour, J. Mabrouki, Y. Farhaoui, and A. Guezzaz, "Experimental evaluation of proposed algorithm for identifying abnormal messages in SIP network," in *Intelligent Systems in Big Data, Semantic Web and Machine Learning*, N. Gherabi and J. Kacprzyk, Eds., in Advances in Intelligent Systems and Computing, vol. 1344. Springer International Publishing, 2021, pp. 1–10. doi: 10.1007/978-3-030-72588-4_1.

21. J. Mabroukı, M. Azrour, A. Boubekraoui, and S. El Hajjaji, "Intelligent system for the protection of people," in *Intelligent Systems in Big Data, Semantic Web and Machine Learning*, Springer, 2021, pp. 157–165.

22. M. Azrour, J. Mabrouki, G. Fattah, A. Guezzaz, and F. Aziz, "Machine learning algorithms for efficient water quality prediction," *Modeling Earth Systems and Environment*, vol. 8, no. 2, pp. 2793–2801, 2022.

23. R. Alekya, N. D. Boddeti, K. S. Monica, R. Prabha, and V. Venkatesh, "IoT based smart healthcare monitoring systems: A literature review," *European Journal of Molecular & Clinical Medicine*, vol. 7, no. 11, p. 2020, 2021.

24. B. Farahani, F. Firouzi, and K. Chakrabarty, "Healthcare iot," in *Intelligent Internet of Things*, Springer, 2020, pp. 515–545.

25. M. Papaioannou et al., "A survey on security threats and countermeasures in internet of medical things (IoMT)," *Transactions on Emerging Telecommunications Technologies*, vol. 33, no. 6, p. e4049, 2022.

26. M. Mushtaq, M. A. Shah, and A. Ghafoor, "The internet of medical things (IOMT): Security threats and issues affecting digital economy," in Proceedings of the Competitive Advantage in the Digital Economy (CADE 2021), pp. 137–142, 2021.

27. R. Somasundaram and M. Thirugnanam, "Review of security challenges in healthcare internet of things," *Wireless Networks*, vol. 27, pp. 5503–5509, 2021.

28. A. Avinashiappan and B. Mayilsamy, "Internet of medical things: Security threats, security challenges, and potential solutions," *Internet of Medical Things: Remote Healthcare Systems and Applications*, pp. 1–16, 2021.

29. N. Garg, M. Wazid, J. Singh, D. P. Singh, and A. K. Das, "Security in IoMT-driven smart healthcare: A comprehensive review and open challenges," *Security and Privacy*, vol. 5, no. 5, p. e235, 2022.

30. J. Chanchaichujit, A. Tan, F. Meng, and S. Eaimkhong, "An introduction to Healthcare 4.0," in *Healthcare 4.0*, Springer Singapore, 2019, pp. 1–15. doi: 10.1007/978-981-13-8114-0_1.

31. M. Wehde, "Healthcare 4.0," *IEEE Engineering Management Review*, vol. 47, no. 3, pp. 24–28, 2019.

32. G. Aceto, V. Persico, and A. Pescapé, "Industry 4.0 and health: Internet of things, big data, and cloud computing for healthcare 4.0," *Journal of Industrial Information Integration*, vol. 18, p. 100129, 2020.

33. F. Shrouf, J. Ordieres, and G. Miragliotta, "Smart factories in Industry 4.0: A review of the concept and of energy management approached in production based on the Internet of Things paradigm," in *2014 IEEE International Conference on Industrial Engineering and Engineering Management*, Dec. 2014, pp. 697–701. doi: 10.1109/IEEM.2014.7058728.

34. A. Botta, W. de Donato, V. Persico, and A. Pescapé, "Integration of cloud computing and Internet of Things: A survey," *Future Generation Computer Systems*, vol. 56, pp. 684–700, Mar. 2016, doi: 10.1016/j.future.2015.09.021.

35. S. Selvaraj and S. Sundaravaradhan, "Challenges and opportunities in IoT healthcare systems: A systematic review," *SN Applied Sciences*, vol. 2, no. 1, pp. 1–8, 2020.

36. R. De Michele and M. Furini, "Iot healthcare: Benefits, issues and challenges," in *Proceedings of the 5th EAI International Conference on Smart Objects and Technologies for Social Good*, 2019, pp. 160–164.

37. M. Shakeri, A. Sadeghi-Niaraki, S.-M. Choi, and S. R. Islam, "Performance analysis of IoT-based health and environment WSN deployment," *Sensors*, vol. 20, no. 20, p. 5923, 2020.

38. M. B. Hassan, R. A. Saeed, O. Khalifa, E. S. Ali, R. A. Mokhtar, and A. A. Hashim, "Green machine learning for green cloud energy efficiency," in *2022 IEEE 2nd International Maghreb Meeting of the Conference on Sciences and Techniques of Automatic Control and Computer Engineering (MI-STA)*, IEEE, 2022, pp. 288–294.

39. M. B. Hassan et al., "Performance evaluation of uplink shared channel for cooperative relay based narrow band Internet of Things network," in *2022 International Conference on Business Analytics for Technology and Security (ICBATS)*, IEEE, 2022, pp. 1–7.

40. E. Bertino and N. Islam, "Botnets and internet of things security," *Computer*, vol. 50, no. 2, pp. 76–79, 2017.

41. S. Dargaoui et al., "An overview of the security challenges in IoT environment," in *Advanced Technology for Smart Environment and Energy*, J. Mabrouki, A. Mourade, A. Irshad, and S. A. Chaudhry, Eds., in Environmental Science and Engineering. Springer International Publishing, 2023, pp. 151–160. doi: 10.1007/978-3-031-25662-2_13.

42. H. Attou, A. Guezzaz, S. Benkirane, M. Azrour, and Y. Farhaoui, "Cloud-based intrusion detection approach using machine learning techniques," *Big Data Mining and Analytics*, vol. 6, no. 3, pp. 311–320, 2023.

43. H. Zhao, P. Bai, Y. Peng, and R. Xu, "Efficient key management scheme for health blockchain," *CAAI Transactions on Intelligence Technology*, vol. 3, no. 2, pp. 114–118, 2018.

44. A. S. Rajasekaran and M. Azees, "An anonymous blockchain-based authentication scheme for secure healthcare applications," *Security and Communication Networks*, vol. 2022, p. e2793116, Feb. 2022, doi: 10.1155/2022/2793116.

45. O. A. Khashan and N. M. Khafajah, "Efficient hybrid centralized and block-chain-based authentication architecture for heterogeneous IoT systems," *Journal of King Saud University - Computer and Information Sciences*, Jan. 2023, doi: 10.1016/j.jksuci.2023.01.011.

46. D. Nigam, S. N. Patel, P. M. D. R. Vincent, K. Srinivasan, and S. Arunmozhi, "Biometric authentication for intelligent and privacy-preserving healthcare systems," *Journal of Healthcare Engineering*, vol. 2022, p. e1789996, Mar. 2022, doi: 10.1155/2022/1789996.

47. K. Chatterjee, A. Singh, Neha, and K. Yu, "A multifactor ring signature based authentication scheme for quality assessment of IoMT environment in COVID-19 scenario," *Journal of Data and Information Quality*, p. 3575811, Jan. 2023, doi: 10.1145/3575811.

48. M. Abdussami, R. Amin, and S. Vollala, "Provably secured lightweight authenticated key agreement protocol for modern health industry," *Ad Hoc Networks*, vol. 141, p. 103094, Mar. 2023, doi: 10.1016/j.adhoc.2023.103094.

CHAPTER 6

Intrusion Detection Framework Using AdaBoost Algorithm and Chi-Squared Technique

Sara Amaouche, Chaimae Hazman, Azidine Guezzaz, Said Benkirane, and Mourade Azrour

6.1 INTRODUCTION

VANET is an important part of intelligent transport systems (ITS) [1], integrating ad-hoc networks, wireless local area networks, and cellular technology to allow different sorts of communication, principally vehicle-to-vehicle (V2V) and vehicle-to-infrastructure (V2I). VANET networks contribute in a major way to better road traffic quality, by limiting the risk of accidents and traffic problems. These advantages do not prevent VANET networks from being vulnerable to many types of attacks. The very high number of vehicles circulating in a VANET network, as well as the rapid typology change due to the nature of VANETs as they contain vehicles with continuous movement, are leading to increasing road congestion issues, resulting in a rapidly increasing frequency of accidents, affecting the safety of human life. Therefore, in order to develop a new

DOI: 10.1201/9781003438779-6

transport system, it is essential to ensure road safety and effective transport control [2]. On this point, security and safety of transportation represent a precondition for the development of a safe smart city [2], [29], [33].

This chapter presents an IDS framework dedicated to VANET networks, using AdaBoost to enhance the rate of detection. Several feature selection techniques have been used, SMOTE to solve the class imbalance problem, Chi-squared for feature selection, and one-shot coding for categorical value conversion. The proposed model was tested on the NSL-KDD, UNSW-NB15, and TON-IOT datasets using the following metrics for evaluation: accuracy, precision, recall, and F1-score. The structure of the rest of this paper is as follows. Section 6.2 covers the related works concerning VANETs. Section 6.3 explains the proposed framework for the classification of attacks that threaten VANET networks. Section 6.4 discusses in detail the simulation results. Finally, Section 6.5 presents the conclusion.

6.2 RELATED WORKS

VANETs are a type of wireless network directly linked to the internet, developed specifically to enhance V2V and V2I communication [3]. VANETs possess distinctive characteristics that set them apart from other wireless network types. Mainly, the high mobility of nodes in VANET [4], as vehicles are continuously moving, leading to an extremely dynamic network topology. As a result, this poses challenges for maintaining strong communication connections among vehicles [4]. The fact that VANETs do not require any infrastructure is also an advantage, as they are generally constructed independently of any infrastructure [5]. VANET networks are based on ad-hoc connectivity, which enables vehicles to exchange data directly with neighboring vehicles or infrastructure elements. Such types of links are quickly broken as vehicles are moving [5]. VANET networks use dedicated short range communication (DSRC) [6], which is a wireless communication based essentially on IEEE 802.11p. DSRC works at a frequency of 5.9 GHz and is dedicated to V2V communication, offering ultra-reliable and lower latency links [6]. The processing capacity, memory, and energy efficiency of vehicles in VANET networks are restricted. Consequently, it is essential to carefully optimize protocols of communication to guarantee optimum use of resources while minimizing their impact on the performance of the vehicle [6]. Despite all these advantages, VANETs face considerable challenges in terms of confidentiality and security, reflecting the sensitivity of the data transmitted [7]. In particular, ensuring the security of communication and safeguarding driver and passenger confidentiality are critical factors in designing a VANET network [7]. When deploying this type of network in urban areas, the fact that they must be scalable to handle greater volumes of vehicles and adapt to changing densities of traffic must be considered. VANETs must also be able to manage time-sensitive communications such as broadcasting urgent messages or avoiding collisions [7]. Reduced-latency communications and robust routing systems are required to guarantee the accurate delivery of time-sensitive data. These features determine the design and functioning of VANET networks, which respond to the specific conditions and requirements of vehicular traffic, allowing a huge variety of uses to improve safety and efficiency as well as the quality of the driving [6]. The use of IDSs [8] in VANET networks represents an important tool for improving the security and robustness of the network. IDSs can identify and address possible vulnerabilities and malevolent activities [34], guaranteeing the integrity and confidentiality of communications [8]. IDSs represent a technology designed to survey traffic on networks to detect any abnormal activities or attempts to gain unauthorized access [14]. IDS's main aim is to identify and react to possible vulnerabilities in real time [9], [19]. Two main types of IDS are available: Network-based IDS (NIDS) [9], which surveys network traffic at special positions on the network, typically on routers or switches. It scans packets and looks for models that identify possible attacks or malware sources. NIDS can identify attacks on more than one system. Host-based IDS (HIDS) [9], which functions on hosts or servers, checks logs. IDSs can identify attacks or illegal operations that may be missed through network surveillance. Strategic placement of IDS sensors within the VANET infrastructure is essential for effective monitoring [10], [37]. These sensors can be strategically positioned at key locations, including roadside units (RSUs) and specific points within the network [10]. This placement enables comprehensive monitoring of both V2V and V2I communication. When determining the placement of IDS sensors, important considerations include network coverage, communication range, and the criticality of network segments [10]. To enhance security in VANETs, it is crucial for IDS systems to analyze network traffic effectively. This involves scrutinizing packet headers, payload data, and communication patterns to identify any irregularities or suspicious patterns that may indicate potential security breaches or attacks. Employing machine learning techniques can be beneficial for the detection of known attack signatures or identifying abnormal behavior [11]. In VANETs, IDS systems can be categorized into two primary types: Signature-based IDS and anomaly-based IDS [12]. Signature-based IDSs rely on a database of pre-defined attack signatures to identify and match patterns of malicious activities. While these systems are effective in detecting known attacks, they may face challenges in detecting novel or zero-day attacks [12]. On the other hand, anomaly-based [35] IDSs establish a baseline of normal behavior and flag any deviations from this baseline as potential anomalies. This type of IDS is suitable for detecting unknown or evolving attacks [36], but it is important to note that it can also generate false positives [12].

Various machine learning (ML) and deep learning (DL) algorithms have utilized IDSs to identify intrusions in VANETs (refer to Figure 6.1). In this study [13], researchers proposed an evaluation model that specifically focuses on ML methods for misbehavior analysis (MA) in VANETs. To assess the effectiveness of ML, they integrated the model-based development (MBD) process into an extended version of the VEINS simulator. The study demonstrated that ML techniques facilitate accurate classification of reported Security Threat Indicators (STIs) and enable the identification of various types of misbehaviors. In this paper [30], authors introduced a multi-decision intelligent detection model named CEAP, specifically designed to accommodate the dynamic nature of VANETs. The model aims to achieve a high detection rate while minimizing overhead. To implement this model, the researchers employed the support vector machine (SVM) technique for classifying vehicles as cooperative or mischievous. In their paper, the researchers presented ML techniques, specifically k-nearest neighbors (KNN) and SVM algorithms, for clustering and classifying intrusions in VANETs. The proposed intrusion detection technique primarily focuses on analyzing the delay and timing ratio of request and reply messages within the controller area network (CAN). In this article [15], a novel intrusion detection model utilizing ML techniques is introduced to enhance the detection rate in the context

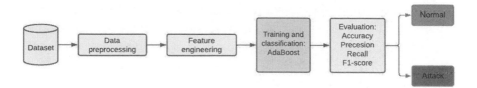

FIGURE 6.1   Scheme of proposed approach

of the Internet of Things (IoT) environment. This research paper [16] introduces a novel intrusion detection approach for securing VANETs by incorporating ML and game theory techniques. The proposed method addresses the security of VANETs from upper units, including roadside units (RSUs) and cluster heads (CHs), down to individual vehicles. The detection of malfunctioning CHs is achieved using an artificial neural network (ANN) implemented in the RSUs, while a real-time SVM is employed for detecting malfunctioning vehicles within the clusters. In their research paper [2], the authors put forward a mechanism utilizing ML to enhance the efficiency of IDS specifically for position tampering attacks. The proposed model was evaluated by comparing two ML methods, namely k-nearest neighbor (KNN) and random forest (RF), which were employed for detecting malicious vehicles. Additionally, an ensemble learning algorithm that combines KNN and RF was utilized to improve the overall detection performance. In the study conducted by researchers [17], an enhanced IDS called DEIGASe is introduced. This IDS utilizes information gain (IG) and genetic algorithms (GA) to select the most relevant features for improved performance. Authors in [18] conducted a study where they integrated RF with forward and reverse ranking feature selection techniques. To ensure data integrity, the KDD-CUP99 dataset underwent thorough cleaning, eliminating any redundant information. The researchers employed various preprocessing methods including normalization, discretization, and balancing. The outcomes revealed that RF-FSR attained an impressive classification accuracy of 99.90%, while RF-BER achieved 99.88%. The authors of [27] developed an enhanced intrusion detection framework for VANETs using feature selection, class imbalance handling, and RF as the classifier. The model achieved exceptional performance with high accuracy, precision, recall, and F1-score, along with a perfect area under the curve (AUC) score on multiple datasets. This paper [28] aims to analyze the various applications, use cases, issues, and challenges of the IoT in smart agriculture, with the ultimate goal of providing guidelines for the development of a tailored intrusion detection system for agricultural networks. This paper [32] presents a novel cloud-based IDS model using RF and feature engineering. The proposed approach achieves high accuracy, precision, and recall, outperforming recent studies on two datasets, Bot-IoT and NSL-KDD, with 98.3% and 99.99% accuracy respectively (Table 6.1).

TABLE 6.1   Classification and comparison studies of some recent researches

References	Used Learning Method	Accuracy (%)	Type
[31]	Threshold	0.98	Multiple Misbehaviors
	N-CTB	0.98	
	CTB	0.99	
	XGBoost	0.98	
	LinearSVC	0.98	
	SVM-SVC	0.98	
	MLP-T1	0.98	
	MLP-T10	0.99	
	LSTM	0.99	
[13]	RF	0.98	Multiple Misbehaviors
	XGboost	0.99	
	LightGBM	0.99	
	Neural networks	0.97	
	LSTM	1	
[30]	Linear kernel	0.98	Multiple Misbehaviors
	Multilayer percepton	0.97	
	kernel	0.98	
	Quadratic kernel	0.98	
	Polynomial kernel	0.98	
	Gaussian radial basis function kernel		
[20]	KNN	0.98	Multiple Misbehaviors
	SVM	0.97	
[16]	Senior2Local	0.98	Multiple Misbehaviors
	SVM-case	0.90	
	CEAP	0.90	
[2]	RF	0.92	Multiple Misbehaviors
	KNN	0.91	

6.3 PROPOSED WORK

In this section, we present our novel IDS designed specifically for VANET networks. Our IDS aims to accurately identify and classify malicious vehicles within the network. To achieve this, we utilize the AdaBoost algorithm for detecting known attacks. Additionally, we optimize the dataset by employing the chi-squared technique for efficient feature selection, reducing computational time and resource requirements. We also address the issue of class imbalance in the datasets by applying the SMOTE technique. Subsequently, the AdaBoost classifier is trained using 15 selected features to establish our robust intrusion detection system. To evaluate the performance of our model, we conduct experiments using three distinct datasets: NSL-KDD, UNSW-NB15, and TON-IOT. The proposed system is visually depicted in Figure 6.1, illustrating three key steps: data preprocessing, feature selection, and classification. In the following section, we will discuss each technique utilized during the development of our IDS in detail.

In order to ensure meaningful analysis, proper processing of the data is essential. In our model, missing values will be replaced with the most recent value. To convert categorical values into numeric ones, we employ the one-hot encoding technique. To address the issue of class imbalance, we utilize the SMOTE technique, an oversampling method that aims to balance the attack class by increasing the minority class, and for feature selection, we use chi-squared.

6.4 EVALUATION STUDY

6.4.1 Environment Description

The NSL-KDD dataset [21] is an enhanced version of the KDD'99 dataset that was specifically created to overcome the limitations associated with it. Several improvements were made to address these limitations. Firstly, redundant data in both the training and test sets were eliminated. Additionally, the records in the KDD'99 dataset were balanced based on their difficulty classification level, resulting in a more useful and relevant dataset for evaluating learning algorithms. These enhancements ensure that the NSL-KDD dataset provides a more effective platform for evaluating the performance of various learning algorithms. A security dataset for computer networks called UNSW-NB15 [22] was released in 2015. The dataset is composed of 2,540,044 realistic modern, normal, and assault actions. The IXIA traffic generator used three servers to gather these recordings. A third server was configured for the collection of abnormal traffic statistics, and two of them were configured for distributing normal traffic. The ToN-IoT dataset [23] contains varied data from numerous sources, including telemetry data, Windows, Linux, and traffic from the network. It was created to investigate and assemble IoT and IIoT data sources. The targeted class comprises nine different types of attacks (XSS, DDoS, DoS, password cracking attacks, recognition or verification, MITM, ransomware, backdoors, and injection attacks), and the information in it is displayed in CSV format with one column categorized as normal or abnormal.

We run our tests on an Intel(R) Core(TM) i7 CPU @ 1.90GHz 2.11 GHz, and 16GB in RAM, with Windows 10 x64-bit. We implemented our model and feature engineering using Python v3.10.6 (Figure 6.2).

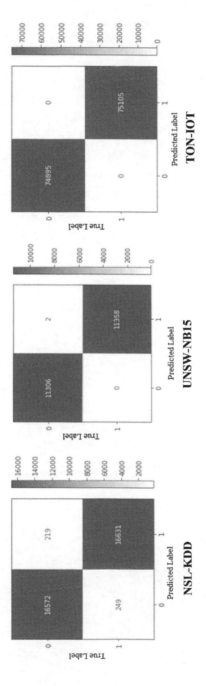

FIGURE 6.2 Confusion matrix of prediction on NSL-KDD, UNSW-NB15, TON-IOT datasets

6.4.2 Discussion of Results

6.4.2.1 Using NSL-KDD Dataset

The results of the class attack before and after implementing the SMOTE technique on the NSL-KDD dataset are depicted in Figures 6.3 and 6.4. The SMOTE technique was employed to address the issue of imbalanced classes within our dataset, as evident in Figure 6.3. By examining the outcomes presented in Figure 6.4, it can be inferred that the application of the SMOTE technique successfully resolved the problem of class imbalance.

To determine the features of our model, we employed the Chi-squared technique. Figure 6.5 displays the outcomes of the influential features identified within our dataset. In constructing our model, we utilized the top 20 features: 'service', 'flag', 'src_bytes', 'dst_bytes', 'logged_in', 'count', 'serror_rate', 'srv_serror_rate', 'same_srv_rate', 'diff_srv_rate', 'srv_diff_host_rate', 'dst_host_count', 'dst_host_srv_count', 'dst_host_same_srv_rate', 'dst_host_diff_srv_rate', 'dst_host_same_src_port_rate', 'dst_host_srv_diff_host_rate', 'dst_host_serror_rate', 'dst_host_srv_serror_rate', 'level'.

Our model employed the AdaBoost classifier and was evaluated on the NSL-KDD dataset. The confusion matrices of the classification results on this dataset presented in Figure 6.2 illustrate that our model achieved

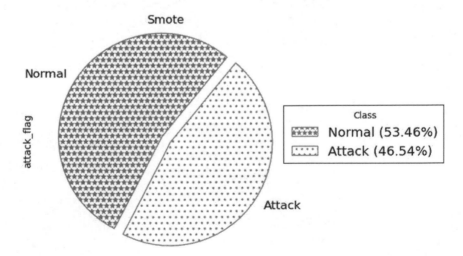

FIGURE 6.3 Diagram of the class of attack before applying the SMOTE technique when using NSL-KDD dataset

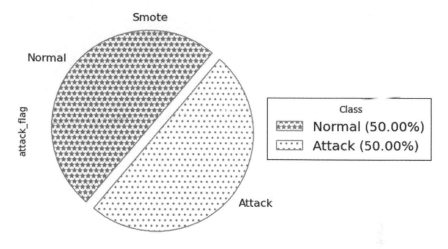

FIGURE 6.4   Diagram of the class of attack after applying the SMOTE technique when using NSL-KDD dataset

exceptional performance with a low false positive rate (FPR) and false negative rate (FNR).

6.4.2.2 Using UNSW-NB15 Dataset

The imbalance of classes within our UNSW-NB15 dataset is evident in Figure 6.6. In order to address this issue, we employed the SMOTE technique, the outcomes of which can be observed in Figure 6.7. Through the application of SMOTE, we successfully achieved balance between the two classes, attack and normal.

To identify the features of our model, we utilized the chi-squared technique. Figure 6.8 illustrates the results of the influential features within our dataset. In constructing our model, we specifically employed the top 20 features: 'id', 'dur', 'state', 'dpkts', 'sbytes', 'dbytes', 'rate', 'sttl', 'dttl', 'sload', 'dload', 'sinpkt', 'dinpkt', 'tcprtt', 'synack', 'ackdat', 'smean', 'dmean', 'ct_state_ttl', 'ct_dst_sport_ltm'.

Furthermore, the confusion matrices of the UNSW-NB15 dataset presented in Figure 6.2 indicate that our model has been successfully constructed with two false positive rates (FPRs) and zero false negative rates (FNRs) (Figure 6.9).

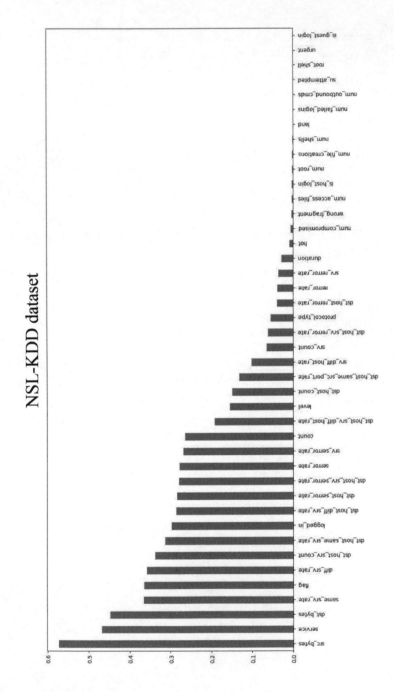

FIGURE 6.5   Feature selection in case of using NSL-KDD dataset

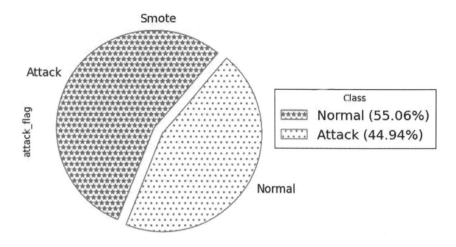

FIGURE 6.6   Diagram of the class of attack before applying the SMOTE technique when using UNSW-NB15 dataset

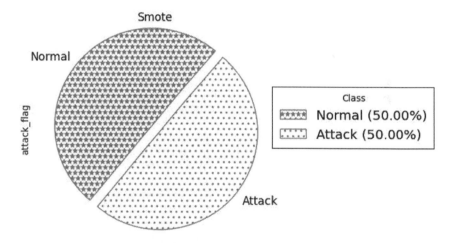

FIGURE 6.7   Diagram of the class of attack after applying the SMOTE technique when using UNSW-NB15 dataset

6.4.2.3 Using TON-IOT Dataset

When working with the TON-IOT dataset, we encountered the common issue of imbalanced classes, as depicted in Figure 6.10. To overcome this challenge, we implemented the SMOTE technique, as shown in Figure 6.11, which successfully balanced the two classes, namely attack and normal.

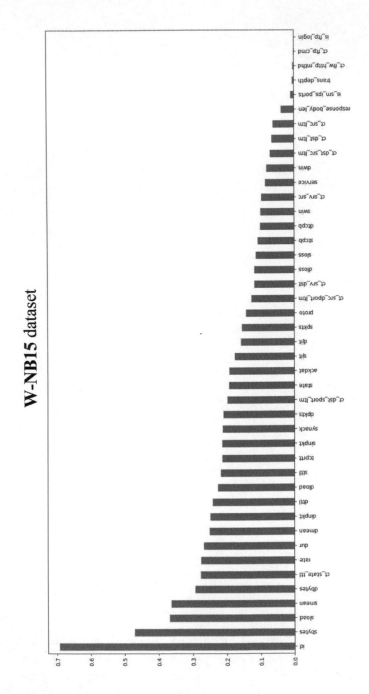

FIGURE 6.8 Feature selection in case of using UNSW-NB15 dataset

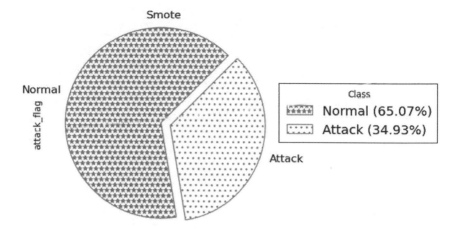

FIGURE 6.9 Diagram of the class of attack before applying the SMOTE technique when using TON-IOT dataset

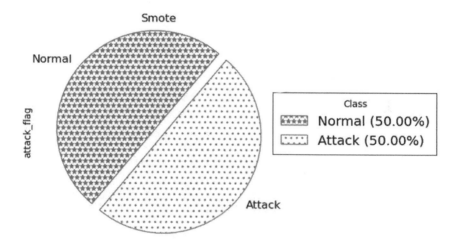

FIGURE 6.10 Diagram of the class of attack after applying the SMOTE technique when using TON-IOT dataset

Upon observing Figure 6.10, it becomes evident that the issue of class imbalance depicted in Figure 6.9 has been effectively addressed through the utilization of the SMOTE technique. The results of the chi-square technique are presented in Figure 6.11, and for our model implementation, we selected the top 20 features: 'ts', 'src_ip', 'src_port', 'dst_ip', 'dst_port', 'proto', 'service', 'duration', 'conn_state', 'dns_AA', 'dns_RD', 'dns_RA', 'dns_rejected', 'weird_name', 'weird_notice', 'label'. With the TON-IOT

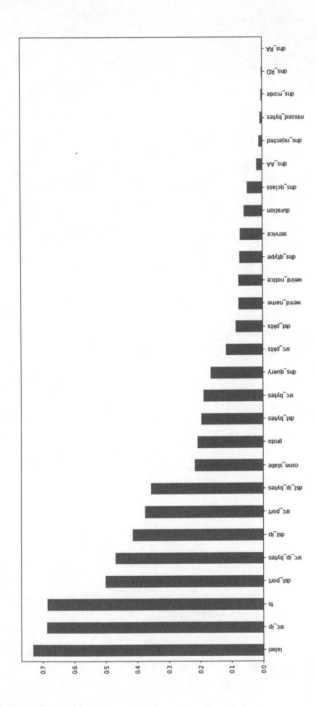

FIGURE 6.11 Feature selection in case of using TON-IOT dataset

dataset, our model achieved satisfactory outcomes. The results showcased in Figure 6.4 demonstrate the excellent performance of our model, attaining 100% accuracy, precision, recall, and F1-score. The provided confusion matrices in Figure 6.4 further emphasize the successful execution of our model, achieving zero false positive rates (FPRs) and zero false negative rates (FNRs).

To conduct a comprehensive comparison, our model underwent testing on three distinct datasets: NSL-KDD, UNSW-NB15, and TON-IOT. Through this evaluation, our model demonstrated remarkable efficiency and achieved a high detection rate. The comparative analysis, as depicted in Table 6.2, along with the accompanying figures, clearly indicates that our proposed model outperforms other IDSs in terms of robustness and execution time. These results reaffirm the superior performance of our model.

TABLE 6.2   Experimentation result on TON-IOT dataset

References	Algorithm	Accuracy	Precision	Recall	F1-Score
[24]	Random Forest	0.96	—	—	0.94
	Bayesian-Coresets	0.82			0.77
	SVM	0.85			0.82
	CNN	0.95			0.93
[25]	Logistic regression	0.66	0.57	0.57	0.57
	Naive Bayes	0.62	0.55	0.55	0.55
	Decision tree	0.88	0.91	0.91	0.91
	Random forest	0.87	0.91	0.91	0.91
	AdaBoost	0.41	0.23	0.23	0.23
	K-nearest Neighbor	0.97	0.97	0.97	0.97
	SVM	0.77	0.75	0.75	0.75
	XGBoost	0.98	0.97	0.97	0.97
[26]	RF	—	0.94	0.93	0.93
	KNN		0.86	0.84	0.85
	Naive Bayes		0.69	0.62	0.62
	Logistic Regression		0.78	0.65	0.65
	Decision Tree		0.93	0.93	0.93
	MLP		0.86	0.76	0.78
	ANN		0.88	0.85	0.86
	CNN		0.87	0.77	0.78
	LSTM		0.93	0.92	0.93
Proposed Model	AdaBoost (with NSL-KDD)	0.987	0.986	0.986	0.986
	AdaBoost (with UNSW-NB15)	0.924	0.999	0.999	0.999
	AdaBoost (TON-IOT)	1	1	1	1

6.5 CONCLUSION

Intrusion detection plays a crucial role in enhancing the effectiveness of security measures to counteract attacks. This study introduces a network-based solution for VANET security in the context of intrusion detection. The research findings, based on diverse datasets, along with a performance comparison, highlight the exceptional efficiency and effectiveness of our proposed model. This study further underscores the significance of AdaBoost as a robust algorithm. Subsequent research endeavors will encompass multi-class classification and the development of an intrusion detection model utilizing deep learning algorithms.

REFERENCES

1. Benamar, M., Benamar, N., Singh, K. D., & El Ouadghiri, D. (2013, May). Recent study of routing protocols in VANET: Survey and taxonomy. In proceeding of *WVNT 1st International Workshop on Vehicular Networks and Telematics*.
2. Ercan, S., Ayaida, M., & Messai, N. (2021). Misbehavior detection for position falsification attacks in VANETs using machine learning. *IEEE Access*, 10, 1893–1904.
3. Sagaama, I., Kchiche, A., Trojet, W., & Kamoun, F. (2023). Energy consumption models in VANET simulation tools for electric vehicles: A literature survey. *International Journal of Ad Hoc and Ubiquitous Computing*, 42(1), 30–46.
4. Erritali, M., & El Ouahidi, B. (2013, April). A survey on VANET intrusion detection systems. In *Proceedings of the 2013 International Conference on Systems, Control, Signal Processing and Informatics* (pp. 16–19).
5. Murugan, S., Jeyalaksshmi, S., Mahalakshmi, B., Suseendran, G., Jabeen, T. N., & Manikandan, R. (2020). Comparison of ACO and PSO algorithm using energy consumption and load balancing in emerging MANET and VANET infrastructure. *Journal of Critical Reviews*, 7(9), 1197–1204.
6. Pramudya, P. B., & Alamsyah, A. (2022). Implementation of signature-based intrusion detection system using SNORT to prevent threats in network servers. *Journal of Soft Computing Exploration*, 3(2), 93–98.
7. Ramalingam, M., & Thangarajan, R. (2020). Mutated k-means algorithm for dynamic clustering to perform effective and intelligent broadcasting in medical surveillance using selective reliable broadcast protocol in VANET. *Computer Communications*, 150, 563–568.
8. Grover, J. (2022). Security of vehicular Ad Hoc networks using blockchain: A comprehensive review. *Vehicular Communications*, 34, 100458.
9. Guezzaz, A., Azrour, M., Benkirane, S., Mohyeddine, M., Attou, H., & Douiba, M. (2022). A lightweight hybrid intrusion detection framework

using machine learning for edge-based IIoT security. *International Arab Journal of Information Technology*, 19(5), 822–830.
10. Sharma, S., & Kaul, A. (2018). A survey on intrusion detection systems and honeypot based proactive security mechanisms in VANETs and VANET cloud. *Vehicular Communications*, 12, 138–164.
11. Guezzaz, A., Asimi, A., Asimi, Y., Tbatou, Z., & Sadqi, Y. (2017). A lightweight neural classifier for intrusion detection. *General Letters in Mathematics*, 2(2), 57–66.
12. Masdari, M., & Khezri, H. (2020). A survey and taxonomy of the fuzzy signature-based intrusion detection systems. *Applied Soft Computing*, 92, Article ID 106301.
13. Mahmoudi, I., Kamel, J., Ben-Jemaa, I., Kaiser, A., & Urien, P. (2020). Towards a reliable machine learning-based global misbehavior detection in C–ITS: Model evaluation approach. In A. Laouiti, A. Qayyum, & M. N. M. Saad, Eds. *Vehicular Ad-Hoc Networks for Smart Cities* (pp. 73–86). Springer.
14. Hazman, C., Benkirane, S., Guezzaz, A., Azrour, M., & Abdedaime, M. (2023). Intrusion detection framework for IoT-based smart environments security. In *Artificial Intelligence and Smart Environment: ICAISE'2022* (pp. 546–552). Springer.
15. Guezzaz, A., Benkirane, S., & Azrour, M. (2022). A novel anomaly network intrusion detection system for Internet of things security. In *IoT and Smart Devices for Sustainable Environment* (pp. 129–138). Springer.
16. Zeng, Y., Qiu, M., Ming, Z., & Liu, M. (2018, December). Senior2local: A machine learning based intrusion detection method for vanets. In *International Conference on Smart Computing and Communication* (pp. 417–426). Springer.
17. Hazman, C., Guezzaz, A., Benkirane, S., & Azrour, M. (2023). Toward an intrusion detection model for IoT-based smart environments. *Multimedia Tools and Applications*, 1–22.
18. Al-Jarrah, O. Y., Siddiqui, A., Elsalamouny, M., Yoo, P. D., Muhaidat, S., & Kim, K. (2014). Machine-learning-based feature selection techniques for large-scale network intrusion detection. In *2014 IEEE 34th International Conference on Distributed Computing Systems Workshops*. IEEE.
19. Hazman, C., Benkirane, S., Guezzaz, A., Azrour, M., & Abdedaime, M. (2023). Building an intelligent anomaly detection model with ensemble learning for IoT-based smart cities. In *Advanced Technology for Smart Environment and Energy* (pp. 287–299). Springer.
20. Alshammari, A., Zohdy, M. A., Debnath, D., & Corser, G. (2018). Classification approach for intrusion detection in vehicle systems. *Wireless Engineering and Technology*, 9(4), 79–94.
21. Dhanabal, L., & Shantharajah, S. P. (2015). A study on NSL-KDD dataset for intrusion detection system based on classification algorithms. *International Journal of Advanced Research in Computer and Communication Engineering*, 4(6), 446–452.

22. Moustafa, N., & Slay, J. (2015, November). UNSW-NB15: A comprehensive data set for network intrusion detection systems (UNSW-NB15 network data set). In *2015 Military Communications and Information Systems Conference (MilCIS)* (pp. 1–6). IEEE.

23. Moustafa, N. (2020). ToN-IoT dataset [Online]. Available: https://cloudstor.aarnet.edu.au/plus/s/ds5zW91vdgjEj9i.

24. Bangui, H., Ge, M., & Buhnova, B. (2021). A hybrid data-driven model for intrusion detection in VANET. *Procedia Computer Science*, 184, 516–523.

25. Gad, A. R., Nashat, A. A., & Barkat, T. M. (2021). Intrusion detection system using machine learning for vehicular ad hoc networks based on ToN-IoT dataset. *IEEE Access*, 9, 142206–142217.

26. Slama, O., Alaya, B., & Zidi, S. (2022). Towards misbehavior intelligent detection using guided machine learning in vehicular ad-hoc networks (VANET). *Inteligencia Artificial*, 25(70), 138–154.

27. Amaouche, S., Guezzaz, A., Benkirane, S., Azrour, M., Khattak, S. B. A., Farman, H., & Nasralla, M. M. (2023). FSCB-IDS: Feature selection and minority class balancing for attacks detection in VANETS. *Applied Sciences*, 13(13), 7488.

28. Mohy-eddine, M., Guezzaz, A., Benkirane, S., & Azrour, M. (2023). IoT-enabled smart agriculture: Security issues and applications. In *Artificial Intelligence and Smart Environment: ICAISE'2022* (pp. 566–571). Springer.

29. Dargaoui, S. et al. (2023). An overview of the security challenges in IoT environment. In J. Mabrouki, A. Mourade, A. Irshad, and S. A. Chaudhry, Eds. *Advanced Technology for Smart Environment and Energy* (pp. 151–160). In *Environmental Science and Engineering*. Springer International Publishing. doi: 10.1007/978-3-031-25662-2_13.

30. Wahab, O. A., Mourad, A., Otrok, H., & Bentahar, J. (2016). CEAP: SVM-based intelligent detection model for clustered vehicular ad hoc networks. *Expert Systems with Applications*, 50, 40–54.

31. Kamel, J., Jemaa, I. B., Kaiser, A., Cantat, L., & Urien, P. (2019, December). Misbehavior Detection in C-ITS: A comparative approach of local detection mechanisms. In *2019 IEEE Vehicular Networking Conference (VNC)* (pp. 1–8). IEEE.

32. Attou, H., Guezzaz, A., Benkirane, S., Azrour, M., & Farhaoui, Y. (2023). Cloud-based intrusion detection approach using machine learning techniques. *Big Data Mining and Analytics*, 6(3), 311–320.

33. Mohy-eddine, M., Benkirane, S., Guezzaz, A., & Azrour, M. (2022). Random forest-based IDS for IIoT edge computing security using ensemble learning for dimensionality reduction. *International Journal of Embedded Systems*, 15(6), 467–474.

34. Hazman, C., Guezzaz, A., Benkirane, S., & Azrour, M. (2022). lIDS-SIoEL: Intrusion detection framework for IoT-based smart environments security using ensemble learning. *Cluster Computing*, 1–15.

35. Douiba, M., Benkirane, S., Guezzaz, A., & Azrour, M. (2022). Anomaly detection model based on gradient boosting and decision tree for IoT environments security. *Journal of Reliable Intelligent Environments*, 1–12.

36. Douiba, M., Benkirane, S., Guezzaz, A., & Azrour, M. (2023). An improved anomaly detection model for IoT security using decision tree and gradient boosting. *The Journal of Supercomputing, 79*(3), 3392–3411.
37. Mohy-eddine, M., Guezzaz, A., Benkirane, S., & Azrour, M. (2023). An efficient network intrusion detection model for IoT security using K-NN classifier and feature selection. *Multimedia Tools and Applications*. doi: 10.1007/s11042-023-14795-2.

A Collaborative Intrusion Detection Approach Based on Deep Learning and Blockchain

Chaimae Hazman, Sara Amaouche,
Mohamed Abdedaime, Azidine Guezzaz,
Said Benkirane, and Mourade Azrour

7.1 INTRODUCTION

The widespread usage of the internet in the current contemporary world facilitates data sharing and interchange. As a result, security becomes a major concern. The majority of data transferred via a network is secure and confidential. A secure mechanism is required to protect this information. Criminals utilize assaults to breach network security and steal information transmitted. The intrusion detection system (IDS) provides network security. An IDS is employed to defend a network from threats. It aids in keeping track of both normal and aberrant network activity. Once a computer system is attacked, the IDS generates an alarm. Signature-based surveillance (SIDS) and anomaly-based detection (AIDS) are two ways of detecting malicious activity. SIDS methods detect harmful

DOI: 10.1201/9781003438779-7

network activity by utilizing a common dataset of detection of intrusion. Trademarks define the sequence of attack in a standard dataset. This dataset is used to examine packets entering the system. If a particular pattern is found, it is considered malicious conduct, and an alarm is sent to the supervisor. Alternatively, the message is regarded as regular and is sent across the entire network. The system is unable to manage unidentified attacks, which is a constraint of SIDS. If an old or out-of-date dataset is used, it lacks the hallmark of unidentified assaults.

Because novel threats emerge in the 21st century, there is a demand for clever and creative IDSs for the exchange of information and cooperation. The nodes in a distributed system may cooperate to exchange information that includes trademark datasets, network assets, attack signatures, and information notifications. The transmission of information amongst endpoints may be jeopardized if an intruder gains access to the system and is able to see all actions and data transfer. A hacker can intercept, change, or destroy data as it travels across the network. To offer security for data shared or transferred inside the network's boundaries, an additional robust approach is necessary. The manipulation of data during node swaps might cause network damage. Hackers can simply alter signatures, datasets, files, records, and other data. Access to information in the hands of a hacker puts the computer system in danger [33–44].

Blockchain is an accepted framework for providing privacy to information shared through distributed nodes on a network [1–4]. It offers a decentralized and shareable structure of data for information sharing in a peer-to-peer network [5]. Another aspect of blockchain is the ability to replicate data across many nodes. Replication of information improves safety, and an individual node cannot serve as the network's bottleneck [6], [7]. Due to its inviolability and consensus protocols that are executed by nodes, blockchain is utilized to improve protection in decentralized IDS networks [8]. Most safety applications use blockchain technology for multi-media and confidential exchange of information [9], [10]. Because of its many benefits, blockchain architecture is now used by the majority of computer applications [11], [12]. Blockchain is being used to improve the effectiveness of several safety applications [13], [14]. Blockchain has recently been employed in areas that include the Internet of Things (IoT) [15], security monitoring [16], monetary services, and a number of other areas [17]. Blockchain is an essential study subject in the building of web apps [18] and computing on clouds 19].

In this study, a blockchain-based system is suggested for exchanging fingerprints of new assaults in a network of nodes. In a hybrid approach, the proposed anomaly attack detection techniques. Identity detection is used to evaluate packets in the system. Alternatively, it is routed to the detection of anomalies process. Identification of anomalies methods examine packets and look for regular activity. If the data is typical, it is forwarded across the system; alternatively, it is transmitted to the blockchain architecture. This structure is in charge of signature generation and dissemination in the network. Blockchain ensures the safety of identities sent across dispersed nodes within a network. Hackers are unable to play with signatures since they are duplicated over an immense amount of nodes within a network. Every single node will utilize the recently created fingerprint to modify the dataset. An upgraded dataset aids in assessing the efficacy of pattern detection. The suggested structure is the first to employ blockchain for signature swapping.

7.2 OVERVIEW

7.2.1 Blockchain Structure

In the year 2008, Nakamoto established the blockchain system as a foundation for Bitcoin for tracking transactions. Every transaction made with Bitcoin offers protection against any assaults.

A blockchain is a linked data structure in which every block of data is divided into two parts: the header and the body. Once in a while, the header section includes an earlier hash, a Merkle Consulting root hash, a date and time stamp, and a difficulty goal. A list of activities appears in the body part. The construction of a blockchain is depicted in Figure 7.1. The primary block is usually used as a genesis block, all blocks are cryptographically connected, and blocks are dispersed over a network of nodes [27], [29].

In addition, every single node in the blockchain network requires an identical block list in order to follow the principles of the technology called blockchain. Whenever the latest block arrives to the network, it broadcasts across all nodes. Each of the nodes validates the newly created block by confirming any transactions in the block using an agreement technique. Evidence of activity and evidence of stake are two consensus techniques used to verify that all endpoints have an identical blockchain list [30], [31].

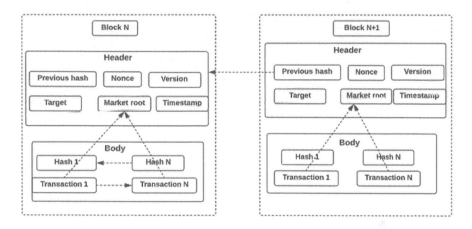

FIGURE 7.1   Blockchain structure

7.2.2 Fundamentals of the Blockchain Technique

There are several blockchain-based ideas utilized on three basic layers of the network, data, and application. Initially the networking layer is peer-to-peer (P2P) network architecture acceptable, which allows for decentralized network links and dispersed network functions. The network layer is in charge of transmitting and validating data throughout nodes. Furthermore, blockchain technology maintains the identical sequence over every point in a network, ensuring that all endpoints are synced (Figure 7.1). As a result, when a new block is created, it is confirmed using an algorithm for consensus. If the latest block is genuine, it will be distributed across all peers. If not, it is discarded. Furthermore, there are numerous varieties of algorithm consensus (Table 7.1), all of which follow the same two principles: (1) The freshness concept supports fair competition by allocating new resources for each new block produced, and (2) the improbability principle prohibits any player from guessing exactly which node will generate the next block.

7.2.3 Long Short-Term Memory (LSTM) Neural Network

LSTM is a method for creating a model with long-term memory while also forgetting irrelevant details in the training data. LSTM differs from traditional RNN in three ways.

There are two distinct kinds of LSTM activation functions: The first is tanh, which happens to be the most often used. It has a result value range of 1 to 1. This function controls networked communication and

TABLE 7.1   Consensus algorithm demonstrations

Algorithm	Overview	Benefit	Drawback
Proof-of-Work (PoW)	To confirm data through difficult mathematical computations, PoW is commonly utilized in blockchain confirmation. The initial node resolves the crypto problem, then creates a fresh block which will subsequently be validated by existing verified nodes in the wider network.	The PoW testing approach is quite effective.	The use of electricity is high.
Proof-of-Stake(PoS)	PoS chooses users depending on their bitcoin stake.	It minimizes PoW energy usage and is suitable for networks with a large-scale networks	It is vulnerable to DoS attacks and lacks coordination among players.
Proof-of Elapsed time (PoET)	It produces time-limited slots for everyone who participates at random, and the person with the least amount of waiting time is included in the next block.	It uses less energy than PoW. It also maintains the concepts of novelty and surprise.	It does not specify how the method will resolve the conflict. Furthermore, its voting procedure is quite difficult.
Proof-of-Space (PoSp)	A validator demands from the provider that a disk space be reserved for storing the necessary data, and then the prover transmits to the validator to guarantee that disk space is reserved.	It minimizes power usage, making it harder for hostile network members to join.	Generating an additional block is complex; hence, addressing the distributed unanimity problem is complicated.
Practical Byzantine Fault	To properly add a new block to the chain, three actions must be completed sequentially: (1) fresh circular, (2) check all information, and (3) broadcast the block to all nodes	It is capable of dealing with a third malicious network.	The node in question is unable to join another network until it has been verified by the entire network.

prevents the rising gradient phenomenon. The tanh function is described as follows:

$$tanh(x) = \frac{e^x - e^{-x}}{e^x + e^{-x}}$$

These sigmoid functions of activation are a second type of activation function. Its outcomes vary from 1 to 1, allowing the neural network's algorithms to eliminate unnecessary input. The following is the definition of the sigmoid function:

$$\sigma(x) = \frac{1}{1 + e^x}$$

Hidden state and cell state: In the standard RNN design, the state that is hidden serves two functions: as the network's memory and as the result of the network's hidden layer of memory. In addition to the hidden metrics, the LSTM networks give a cell status. The hidden state of cells in RNN functions as a short-term memory for working purposes, whereas the cell state in LSTM acts as a long-term memory for storing relevant historical data.

7.2.3.1 Gates

In LSTM, the status's values may be changed via methods known as gates. The LSTM has four gates, as shown in Figure 7.2: the gate that forgets f, the admission gate i, the cell status candidacy gate c, and the outcome gate o. [32] has further information about these gates.

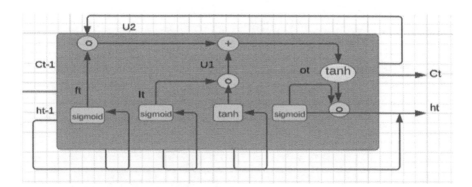

FIGURE 7.2   The LSTM cell structure

7.3 REVIEW AND RELATED WORKS

Multiple methods are currently being developed and put into effect to safeguard the IoT from intrusions and assaults, but they remain insufficient due to difficulties such as speed of response, delay, and enormous information size. To protect fog and cloud in IoT environments, it is required to augment safeguards; Software-Defined Networking (SDN), blockchain, and IDS are examples of emerging technologies, as are Machine Learning (ML) and Deep Learning (DL) algorithms [20]. The IDS has been one of the most successful approaches to tracking network activities and identifying vulnerable endpoints. Scientists have realized that blockchain has tremendous potential to address the issues of establishing confidence across networks while dispersing assaults. This identification-based technique's goal is to detect and restrict offenders. IDSs monitor network transmissions and assess if they are malicious attacks. Furthermore, IDSs can be improved with ML and DL algorithms. It also helps to design preventative systems by recognizing the type of assault [21]. Several new studies suggested the use of blockchain to strengthen IDSs and enhance detection of attacks. The integration of IDSs, blockchain, and ML requires countering network assaults and flaws while also protecting crucial healthcare data. The background of networked systems for intrusion detection is extensive; academics have worked to enhance the safety of decentralized and distributed networks by coordinating with numerous IDSs; however, this past is not particularly relevant to today's growth of the IoT. In 2018 [22] examined the junction of digital currencies and Collaborative Intrusion Detection in Cloud Systems (CIDS) on the same study axis. They presented a framework for implementing digital currencies into CIDS, utilizing the technology as a way to enhance monitoring trust. Hu et al. [23] developed an entirely novel CIDS methodology based on blockchain for distributed intrusion detection in Multimicrogrid (MMG) systems in 2019. The blockchain agreement method and incentive systems are employed to provide CIDS without the need for a central management or trustworthy authority. According to Li et al. [24], Collaborative Blockchained Signature-Based Intrusion Detection System (CBSigIDS) is a general design of cooperative blockchain signature-based IDSs that build and maintain an established signature in an interconnected IoT network. CBSigIDS provides an accurate detection mechanism in distributed systems that is robust and effective without the need for a trusted intermediary. [25] proposed a distributed CIDS in 2019 where any IDS safely sends trusted data regarding outside networks and hosts to other CIDS members. This data is aggregated securely depending on source trustworthiness, calculated according to issue replies, and stored on a blockchain. Alkadi et al. [26] launched a CIDS aiming to enable privacy and security in IoT networks using distributed intrusion detection and a blockchain with intelligent contracts in 2020. A simultaneous long-term memory DL algorithm (BiLSTM) detects intrusions. Li et al. [28] recently proposed a novel architecture of blockchain-based cooperative intrusion detection in SDN Blockchain-Based Collaborative Intrusion Detection in Software Defined Networking (BlockCIDSDN) that enhances resilience and safety by merging SDN, CIDS, and blockchain in the year 2022. The results demonstrated the method's validity and usefulness in rejecting threats from within, boosting alarm aggregate resilience, and saving bandwidth on networks.

7.4 PROPOSAL MODEL

The goal of our suggested strategy is to safeguard smart cities by safeguarding nodes in the case of an unlawful assault through the integration of IDS in smart cities. An IDS is an efficient safety tool that might be upgraded using ML and DL algorithms; nevertheless, since smart cities are scattered, one IDS is insufficient to adequately recognize diverse

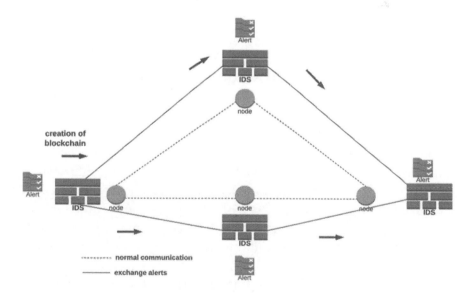

FIGURE 7.3 The suggested method for cooperative intrusion detection

assaults. Actually, we propose an interactive distributed smart cities-based IDS that employs DL approaches with the successful LSTM to develop an intrusion detection system that recognizes attacks at every node, as well as BT to transfer and safeguard attacks identified by points in complete security, as well as to guarantee confidence and dependability between nodes. Furthermore, using the GPU to gain advantages from the LSTM model allows for faster capture identification and computation time (Figure 7.3).

7.5 CONTRIBUTION

For improved security, the IDS ought to be used at every component in the IoT environment to observe network activity and identify nodes that have been abused. Cooperative detection of intrusions encourages IDS nodes to share essential data with one another in order to increase detecting abilities. In contrast, the blockchain is seen as a translucent, dispersed, decentralized, and ordered record. Blockchain technologies have lately proved their value in assuring reliability and confidence in decentralized networks due to the way they work. It is an effective solution to overcome the core difficulties of CIDS since, due to its decentralized structure, it substitutes central handling with a safe cooperative process. When the blockchain is created, the analysis nodes are going to possess the computing capacity they need to calculate and deal with the information, yet they are also capable of serving as tracking units that monitor and transmit the alert. Since all nodes in the distributed ledger network alert recognition and administration, all nodes act entirely as tracking and analyzing units. Each alarm identified by an IDS is recorded in a public blockchain under our proposal. Following that, using the blockchain idea with peer-to-peer construction, each alert produced has to be broadcast and discussed with every other node in order to guarantee that all assaults are transmitted. Alerts on the blockchain are organized within blocks. Every block contains alerts as well as past and current hashes. The hash of the information contained in the block functions similarly to a hallmark key. Every record is cryptographically linked by the hash. The initial block is the Genesis Block. Each component is reliant on the previous one. In order to collaborate, the blockchain is passed on among several nodes.In addition, the sharing of alerts enables the assessment of the dependability of other nodes in the network. As a result, it has the potential to improve the confidence assessment process.

REFERENCES

1. M. Ahmed, A.N. Mahmood, H. Jiankun, A survey of network anomaly detection techniques. *Journal of Network and Computer Applications* 60, 19–31 (2016). https://doi.org/10.1016/j.jnca.2015.11.016

2. J. Manan, A. Ahmed, I. Ullah, L.M. Boulahia, D. Gaiti, Distributed intrusion detection scheme for next generation networks. *Journal of Network and Computer Applications* 147, 102422 (2019). https://doi.org/10.1016/j.jnca.2019.102422

3. P.J. Taylor, T. Dargahi, A. Dehghantanha, R.M. Parizi, K.R. Choo, A systematic literature review of blockchain cyber security. *Digital Communications and Networks* 6(2), 147–156 (2020).

4. D. Berdik, S. Otoum, N. Schmidt, D. Porter, Y. Jararweh, A survey on blockchain for information systems management and security. *Information Processing and Management* 58(1), 102397 (2021). https://doi.org/10.1016/j.ipm.2020.102397

5. Y. He, H. Li, X. Cheng, Y. Liu, C. Yang, L. Sun, A blockchain based truthful incentive mechanism for distributed P2P applications. *IEEE Access* 6, 27324–27335 (2018). https://doi.org/10.1109/ACCESS.2018.2821705

6. T. Dinh, R. Liu, M. Zhang, G. Chen, B. Ooi, J. Wang, Untangling blockchain: A data processing view of blockchain systems. *IEEE Transactions on Knowledge and Data Engineering* 30(7), 1366–1385 (2018). https://doi.org/10.1109/TKDE.2017.2781227

7. M. Miraz, M. Ali, Applications of blockchain technology beyond cryptocurrency. *Annals of Emerging Technologies in Computing* 2(1), 1–6 (2018).

8. W. Meng, E. Tischhauser, Q. Wang, Y. Wang, J. Han, When intrusion detection meets blockchain technology: A review. *IEEE Access* 6(1), 10179–10188 (2018). https://doi.org/10.1109/ACCESS.2018.2799854

9. N. Kumar, S. Aggarwal, Core components of blockchain. In S. Aggarwal, N. Kumar, & P. Raj (Eds.), *Advances in Computers*. Academic Press (2020). https://doi.org/10.1016/bs.adcom.2020.08.010

10. M. Jan, J. Cai, X. Gao, F. Khan, S. Mastorakis, M. Usman, M. Alazab, P. Watters, Security and blockchain convergence with internet of multimedia things: Current trends, research challenges and future directions. *Journal of Network and Computer Applications* 175, 102918 (2021). https://doi.org/10.1016/j.jnca.2020.102918

11. A. Ramachandran, M. Kantarcioglu, *Using Blockchain and Smart Contracts for Secure Data Provenance Management*. arXiv:1709.10000 (2017).

12. K. Toyoda, P. Mathiopoulos, I. Sasase, T. Ohtsuki, A novel blockchain-based product ownership management system (POMS) for anti counterfeits in the post supply chain. *IEEE Access* 5, 17465–17477 (2017). https://doi.org/10.1109/ACCESS.2017.2720760

13. B.T. Rao, V.L. Narayana, V. Pavani, P. Anusha, Use of blockchain in malicious activity detection for improving security. *International Journal of Advanced Science and Technology* 29(3), 9135–9146 (2020).

14. A.R. Mathew, Cyber security through blockchain technology. *International Journal of Engineering and Advanced Technology* 9(1), 3821–3824 (2019).

15. J. Sengupta, S. Ruj, S. Bit, A comprehensive survey on attacks, security issues and blockchain solutions for IoT and IIoT. *Journal of Network and Computer Applications* 149, 102481 (2020). https://doi.org/10.1016/j.jnca .2019.102481

16. C. Liang, B. Shanmugam, S. Azam, A. Karim, A. Islam, M. Zamani, S. Kavianpour, N. Idris, Intrusion detection system for the internet of things based on blockchain and multi-agent systems. *Electronics* 9(7), 1120 (2020). https://doi.org/10.3390/electronics9071120

17. T. Golomb, Y. Mirsky, Y. Elovici. CIoTA: Collaborative IoT anomaly detection via blockchain. arXiv:1803.03807v2, [cs.CY] (2018).

18. N. Agarwal, S. Hussain, A closer look at intrusion detection system for web applications. *Security and Communication Networks* 2018, 9601357 (2018). https://doi.org/10.1155/2018/9601357

19. H. Hamad, M. Al-Hoby, Managing intrusion detection as a service in cloud networks. *International Journal of Computers and Applications* 41(1), 35–40 (2012).

20. Mr. Sankarappa Hareesh, Securing data in health care with block chain. *Journal of Engineering Sciences* 12(8) (August 2021). ISSN NO:0377- 9254.

21. L. Prokhorenkova, G. Gusev, A. Vorobev, et al., CatBoost: Unbiased boosting with categorical features, proceedings of the 32nd international conference on neural information processing systems (2018).

22. N. Alexopoulos, E. Vasilomanolakis, N.R. Ivánkó, M. Mühlhäuser, Towards BlockchainBased collaborative intrusion detection systems. In G. D'Agostino, & A. Scala (Eds.), *Lecture Notes in Computer Science. CRITIS 2017*. Critical Information Infrastructures Security. CRITIS 2017. Lecture Notes in Computer Science, vol. 10707. Springer (2018).

23. B. Hu, C. Zhou, Y. Tian, Y. Qin, X. Junping, A collaborative intrusion detection approach using blockchain for multimicrogrid systems. In *IEEE Transactions on Systems, Man, and Cybernetics: Systems* 49(8), 1720–1730 (August 2019).

24. W. Li, S. Tug, W. Meng, Y. Wang, Designing collaborative blockchained signature-based intrusion detection in IoT environments. *Future Generation Computer Systems* 96, 481–489 (2019) ISSN 0167-739X

25. N. Kolokotronis, S. Brotsis, G. Germanos, C. Vassilakis, S. Shiaeles, On blockchain architectures for trust-based collaborative intrusion detection. In *2019 IEEE World Congress on Services (Services)*, pp. 21–28 (2019).

26. O. Alkadi, N. Moustafa, B. Turnbull, K.-K.R. Choo, A deep blockchain framework enabled collaborative intrusion detection for protecting IoT and cloud networks. *IEEE Internet of Things Journal* 8(12), 9463–9472 (June 15, 2021).

27. H. Attou, A. Guezzaz, S. Benkirane, M. Azrour, Y. Farhaoui, Cloud-based intrusion detection approach using machine learning techniques. *Big Data Mining and Analytics* 6(3), 311–320 (2023).

28. L.I. Wenjuan, W.A.N.G. Yu, M.E.N.G. Weizhi, L.I. Jin, S.U. Chunhua, C.S.D.N. Block, Towards blockchain-based collaborative intrusion detection in software defined networking. *IEICE Transactions on Information and Systems* E105(D2), 272–279, Released on J-STAGE February 1, 2022, Online ISSN 1745-1361, Print ISSN 0916-8532. https://doi.org/10.1587/transinf

29. W. Gao, W.G. Hatcher, W. Yu, A survey of Blockchain: Techniques, applications, and challenges. In *2018 27th International Conference on Computer Communication and Networks (ICCCN)*. IEEE, pp. 1–11 (2018).

30. X. Liang, S. Shetty, D. Tosh, C. Kamhoua, K. Kwiat, L. Njilla, Provchain: A Blockchain-based data provenance architecture in cloud environment with enhanced privacy and availability. In *Proceedings of the 17th IEEE/ACM Int. sym. on Cluster, Cloud and Grid Computing*, pp. 468–477 (2017).

31. M. Muzammal, Q. Qu, B. Nasrulin, Renovating Blockchain with distributed databases: An open-source system. *Future Generation Computer Systems* 90(Supplement C), 105–117 (2019).

32. J. Moedjahedy, A. Setyanto, F.K. Alarfaj, M. Alreshoodi, CCrFS: Combine correlation features selection for detecting phishing Websites using machine learning. *Future Internet* 14(8), 229 (2022).

33. A. Hazman, S. Guezzaz, M. Benkirane, M. Azrour, IDS-SIoEL: Intrusion detection framework for IoT-based smart environments security using ensemble learning. *Cluster Computing* 546–552 (2022).

34. C. Hazman, S. Benkirane, A. Guezzaz, M. Azrour, M. Abdedaime, Intrusion detection framework for IoT-based smart environments security. In *Book Artificial Intelligence and Smart Environment: ICAISE' 2022*. Springer International Publishing, pp. 546–552 (2023).

35. C. Hazman, S. Benkirane, A. Guezzaz, M. Azrour, M. Abdedaime, Building an intelligent anomaly detection model with ensemble learning for IoT-based smart cities. In *Book Advanced Technology for Smart Environment and Energy* (2023).

36. M. Abdedaime, C. Hazman, A. Qafas, M. Jerry, A. Guezzaz. AI applications in smart cities between advantages and security challenge. *Book Artificial Intelligence and Smart Environment: ICAISE' 2022*. Springer International Publishing, pp. 144–155 (2023).

37. A. Guezzaz, S. Benkirane, M. Azrour, A novel anomaly network intrusion detection system for Internet of things security. In *IoT and smart devices for sustainable environment*. Cham: Springer International Publishing, pp. 129–138 (2022).

38. A. Guezzaz, A. Asimi, Y. Asimi, M. Azrour, S. Benkirane, A distributed intrusion detection approach based on machine learning techniques for a cloud security. Intelligent systems in big data, semantic web and machine learning. In *Advances in Intelligent Systems and Computing*. Springer, vol. 1344, pp. 85–94 (2021).

39. S. Amaouche et al., FSCB-IDS: Feature selection and minority class balancing for attacks detection in VANETS. *Applied Sciences*, vol. 13, no. 13, p. 7488 (2023).

40. M. Mohy-eddine, A. Guezzaz, S. Benkirane, M. Azrour, An efficient network intrusion detection model for IoT security using K-NN classifier and feature selection. *Multimedia Tools and Applications* (2023). https://doi.org/10.1007/s11042-023-14795-2

41. M. Mohy-eddine, S. Benkirane, A. Guezzaz, M. Azrour, Random forest-based IDS for IIoT edge computing security using ensemble learning for dimensionality reduction. *International Journal of Embedded Systems* 15(6), 467–474, (2022).

42. M. Douiba, S. Benkirane, A. Guezzaz, M. Azrour, Anomaly detection model based on gradient boosting and decision tree for IoT environments security. *Journal of Reliable Intelligent Environments*, 1–12 (2022).

43. M. Douiba, S. Benkirane, A. Guezzaz, M. Azrour, An improved anomaly detection model for IoT security using decision tree and gradient boosting. *The Journal of Supercomputing*, 79(3), 3392–3411 (2023).

44. M. Mohy-eddine, A. Guezzaz, S. Benkirane, M. Azrour, IoT-enabled smart agriculture: Security issues and applications. In *Artificial Intelligence and Smart Environment: ICAISE'2022*. Springer, pp. 566–571 (2023).

CHAPTER 8

GVGB-IDS: An Intrusion Detection System Using Graphic Visualization and Gradient Boosting for Cloud Monitoring

Hanaa Attou, Hasna Hissou, Azidine Guezzaz, Said Benkirane, and Mourade Azrour

8.1 INTRODUCTION

In today's digital landscape, cyber security has become increasingly crucial as organizations face a rising tide of cyber threats and attacks [1]. The prevalence of data breaches and the potential for financial loss, reputational damage, and privacy violations emphasize the utmost importance of robust security measures [1]. Moreover, CC is a transformative technology [2], [3]. It offers unparalleled scalability, cost-effectiveness, and flexibility for organizations across various sectors [2], [3]. By leveraging CC, businesses can optimize their operations, enhance collaboration, and achieve greater agility [2], [3], [4]. However, the inherent shared infrastructure and network connectivity of cloud environments introduce security challenges that must be addressed to protect sensitive data and ensure the integrity of systems [4], [5]. The Intrusion Detection System (IDS) is essential for preserving the integrity and security of computer networks [4], [5]. IDS solutions monitor network traffic, detect suspicious activities, and alert administrators to potential security breaches [6], [7]. By identifying and responding to intrusions, IDS helps organizations mitigate the impact of cyber-attacks, protect valuable data, and ensure the continuous availability of services [6–8]. To further strengthen security measures, machine learning (ML) and ensemble learning have emerged as powerful tools in cybersecurity [8]. ML algorithms can analyze vast amounts of data and detect attacks to identify malicious activities. In the context of IDS, ML techniques can enhance the accuracy (ACC) of detection, enable proactive threat response, and adapt to evolving attack vectors [7–9]. In this regard, we present an enhanced system applying Graphic Visualization (GV) and Gradient Boosting (GB) to enhance the capabilities of IDS within cloud environments. By integrating GV techniques, the proposed approach aims to improve feature selection, allowing for the identification of relevant and discriminative features for accurate intrusion detection. Additionally, the use of GB, a powerful ensemble-learning algorithm, enhances the IDS's effectiveness by constructing a robust classifier. The combination of these techniques addresses the weaknesses of traditional IDSs and aims to enhance the detection of ACC and recall in cloud environments. Experiments are carried out using the CICIDS 2017 dataset, to assess the efficacy of the suggested approach. The results obtained demonstrate the improved detection capabilities and performance metrics, such as ACC, precision, and recall.

This paper is structured as follows. Section two demonstrates the Cloud Computing (CC) architectures, IDS, and ML algorithms used to detect intrusion. Section three highlights our novel system. In Section four, the experimental environment is illustrated. The collected results are then discussed in section five. The conclusion and next steps are then presented.

8.2 BACKGROUND AND RELATED WORKS

This section presents a state-of-the-art overview of CC architectures, intrusion detection approaches, and ML techniques that are relevant to our research on securing data in the cloud using IDS.

CC has revolutionized the IT industry by offering a range of service models, such as Infrastructure as a Service (IaaS), Platform as a Service (PaaS), and Software as a Service (SaaS) [2], [3], [10], [11]. IaaS enables enterprises to scale resources as needed by offering virtualization, such as virtual machines and storage space, allowing organizations to scale resources as needed [10], [11]. PaaS provides platforms for development and deployment, allowing developers to concentrate on creating applications. SaaS provides ready-to-use software applications [3], [11]. CC provides organizations with scalability, cost-efficiency, and agility, enabling them to meet dynamic business requirements [3], [10], [11]. However, despite its advantages, CC poses security challenges. The shared infrastructure and network connectivity increase the attack surface and service interruptions [3], [12]. Therefore to protect sensitive data, organizations must establish strong security procedures, maintain privacy, and ensure the availability and integrity of their cloud-based services [12]. Therefore, IDS is one of the robust security measures that plays a critical role in safeguarding computer networks against security threats. TheIDS monitors network traffic, system logs, and events to detect suspicious activities and potential security breaches [4], [5]. By analyzing network packets and comparing them against known attack signatures or abnormal behavior, the IDS can identify and alert administrators about potential threats in real time [6], [7]. However, IDS has its limitations. Traditional IDS relies heavily on predefined signatures or rules, often inadequate to detect new and evolving threats [6]. Zero-day attacks and sophisticated malware can bypass traditional IDSs, resulting in undetected intrusions [7]. Additionally, the increasing volume and complexity of network data make it challenging for manual rule creation and analysis. In this regard, ML techniques offer a promising solution to enhance IDS capabilities. ML algorithms can analyze large-scale and high-dimensional data, identify complex patterns, and detect anomalies that may indicate malicious activities [7], [11], [12]. ML-based IDSs can learn from historical data, adapt to new attack vectors, and improve detection ACC [12–16]. In this context, some studies have developed IDSs by employing ML and ensemble-learning algorithms. In 2023, H. Attou et al. [16] proposed a novel model for intrusion detection. This model uses GV to choose the most important features and a Random Forest (RF) classifier to detect attacks. To evaluate this study the NSL-KDD and BoT-IoT datasets were used achieving 98.3 and 100% of ACC respectively. In [17], authors suggested an IDS using RF for security detection and correlation coefficients for feature selection. Their acquired findings on both used datasets are shown in Table 8.1. Authors in [18] proposed a novel model to secure the IoT from intrusion. They use K- Nearest Neighbor (KNN) and Principal Component Analyses (PCA). Their model

TABLE 8.1   A comparison of the most recent works

References	Year	Methods	Datasets	Accuracy (%)
[16]	2023	RF	NSL-KDD	98.3
			BoT-IoT	100
[17]	2022	RF	BoT-IoT	99.99
			wustl_iiot_2021	99.12
[18]	2022	KNN	NSL-KDD	99.1
			BoT-IoT	99.2
[19]	2023	KNN	BoT-IoT	99.99
[20]	2022	AdaBoost	IoT-23	99.9
			BoT-IoT	
			Edge-IIoT	
[21]	2022	GB	NSL-KDD	99.9
		DT	BoT-IoT	
			IoT-23	
			Edge-IIoT	
[22]	2018	LSTM	NSL-KDD	98.4

achieves NSL-KDD and BoT-99.1% and 98.2% of ACC, respectively. In 2023, M. Mohy-eddine et al. suggested efficient intrusion detection for IoT security based on the KNN classifier and feature selection. The model achieves on the Bot-IoT dataset 99.99% of ACC. In (20), the authors suggested a novel system to secure the IoT based on the AdaBoost classifier. The model achieves 99.9% of ACC on three datasets. In 2022, authors in [21] proposed an efficient IDS to secure the IoT. They apply GB and Decision Tree (DT) to detect intrusion. The results obtained demonstrate how well this model performs. In 2018, authors in [22] applied Long Short Term Memory (LSTM), a Deep Learning (DL), algorithm for intrusion detection. They evaluate their model using NSL-KDD.

8.3 OUR PROPOSED MODEL

In this research, we propose the integration of ML techniques, specifically GV and GB, to enhance IDS capabilities within cloud environments as presented in Figure 8.1.

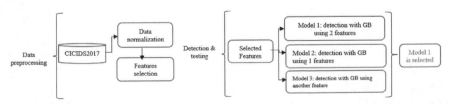

FIGURE 8.1   Diagram of the suggested IDS

Through the integration of ML techniques with IDS, this research aims to address the limitations of traditional IDSs and provide a proactive and efficient approach to secure data in cloud environments. By integrating GV and GB algorithms.

- Firstly, after the preprocessing phase, GV techniques will be employed to visually represent the complex network traffic data. Visualizations will provide valuable insights into the relationships between features and aid in identifying patterns and anomalies. This visual exploration will facilitate the selection of relevant features and improve the understanding of the underlying network behavior, leading to more effective detection of intrusions.

- Secondly, the GB algorithm will be utilized as the core ML technique for intrusion detection tested on a different subset. GB is a powerful ensemble-learning algorithm that combines weak classifiers, in the form of decision trees, to create a strong and accurate classifier. It iteratively builds a series of decision trees, with each subsequent tree focusing on correcting the errors made by the previous ones. This iterative process results in a robust model that can effectively capture complex relationships and distinguish between normal and malicious network traffic.

The combination of GV and GB offers several advantages. Visualizations help in identifying relevant features and reducing the dimensionality of the dataset, enabling more efficient and accurate training of the GB model. Furthermore, visualization aids in interpretability, allowing analysts to gain an understanding of how decisions are made in the process of the IDS and understand the factors contributing to the classification results. By integrating these techniques, the proposed model aims to enhance ACC.

8.4 EXPERIMENTAL SETTING

We use a computer outfitted with a Core TM- i5 8250U CPU clocked at 1.8 GHz and 12 GB of RAM, and our investigation is carried out and evaluated in an experimental setting. After features are condensed using the GB classifier is implemented in Python 3. The proposed model will be implemented and evaluated using the CICIDS 2017 dataset, following the methodology outlined earlier. The performance of the model will be assessed based on various metrics, including ACC, precision, and recall. Therefore, based on recent studies we select the variables to use in our novel system. Firstly, the selected variables from the other studies are the **"Total Length of Fwd Packets"**, **"Flow Duration"**, **"Active Mean"**, **"ActiveStd"**, **"Active Min"**, and **"Active Max"**.

According to the following figures we select the best variables for our study.

- As shown in Figure 8.2, we can detect the type of activity based on the information extracted from the Total Length of Fwd Packets. If the Total Length of Fwd Packets > 0 we have a BENIGN activity.

- According to Figure 8.3, we can detect intrusion if the Flow Duration variable > 0.8.

- Focusing on GV obtained in Figure 8.4, we can conclude that if we have 0.6 < Active Mean < 0.1 we can't confirm if the confronted activity is BENIGN. Their obtained figures are similar to Figure 4 for the rest of the variables.

- Then we conclude that the selected variables are 2: **"Total Length of Fwd Packets"** and **"Flow Duration"**.

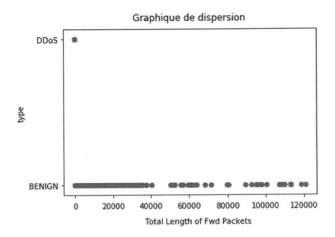

FIGURE 8.2   GV of Total Length of Fwd Packets and variable type

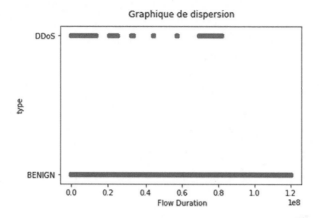

FIGURE 8.3   GV of Flow Duration and variable type

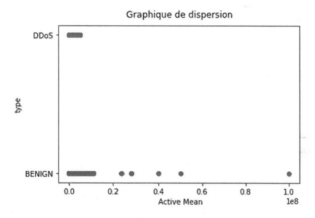

FIGURE 8.4   GV of Active Mean and variable type

8.5 RESULTS AND DISCUSSIONS

This section discusses the results obtained from the experiments conducted to evaluate the proposed model for securing data in cloud environments. The performance of the model is analyzed and discussed, along with relevant insights and observations.

Table 8.2 shows the obtained results of the three models.

TABLE 8.2   Obtained results on CICIDS 2017 dataset

Proposed Models	ACC (%)	Precision (%)	Recall (%)
Model 1: "Total Length of Fwd Packets" and "Flow Duration"	99.99	99.99	99.99
Model 2: Total Length of Fwd Packets	98.7	99	99
Model 3: Flow Duration	79.2	81	78

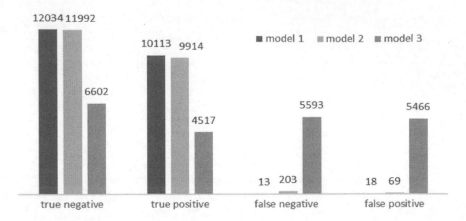

FIGURE 8.5 Performance and the comparison of the three proposed models

- Model 1 showcases exceptional performance, with an ACC of 99.99% and precision and recall values of 99.99%. These results indicate a highly accurate and reliable IDS in securing data within cloud environments. The model effectively classifies network traffic instances as either normal or malicious with minimal misclassifications, ensuring the robustness and efficiency of the proposed approach.

- Model 2 achieves 98.7% of ACC, 99% of precision, and 99 % of recall. But model 1 is still the best if we compare the outcomes shown in Table 8.2 and Figure 8.5.

- Model 3 achieves weak performances based on Table 8.2 and Figure 8.5.

According to Figure 8.5, we conclude that model 1 and model 2 give the best performances in terms of true negative, true positive, false negative, and false positive. In addition to the suppression of Model 3.

8.6 CONCLUSION

In conclusion, this study proposed an enhanced approach to enhance intrusion detection in cloud environments using a combination of GV and GB. The integration of these techniques offers improved ACC, efficiency, and interpretability in detecting intrusions and securing data in the cloud. The obtained results demonstrated the effectiveness of the suggested model in accurately differentiating between normal and malicious network traffic. The findings highlight the importance of leveraging GV to gain insights into complex network behavior and aid in feature selection for intrusion detection. Additionally, the application of GB as a powerful ML algorithm enhances the model's ability to capture intricate relationships and detect intrusions with high precision. Future work in this area can focus on several directions. Firstly, exploring different visualization techniques and algorithms to further enhance the interpretability and usability of the proposed model. Additionally, investigating advanced feature selection methods helps to refine the model's performance and reduce false positives.

REFERENCES

1. O.V. Sviatun, O.V. Goncharuk, C. Roman, O. Kuzmenko and I.V. Kozych. Combating cybercrime: Economic and legal aspects. *WSEAS Transactions on Business and Economics*, vol. 18, p. 751–762, 2021.
2. Q. Zhang, L. Cheng, and R. Boutaba. Cloud computing: State-of-the-art and research challenges. *J. Internet Serv. Appl.*, vol. 1, pp. 7–18, 2010.
3. A. Singh and K. Chatterjee. Cloud security issues and challenges: A survey. *Journal of Network and Computer Applications*, vol. 79, pp. 88–115, 2017.
4. A. Aqas, A. Rasool, A.R. Javed, T. Baker and Z. Jalil. Article cyber security in IoT-based cloud computing: A comprehensive survey. *Electronics*, vol. 11, no. 1, p. 16, 2021.
5. P. S. Gowr and N. Kumar. Cloud computing security: A survey. *International Journal of Engineering and Technology*, vol. 7, no. 2, pp. 355–357, 2018.
6. A. Khraisat, I. Gondal, P. Vamplew and J. Kamruzzaman. Survey of intrusion detection systems: Techniques, datasets and challenges. In *Cybersecurity*. Springer, vol. 2, no. 1, pp. 1–22, 2019.
7. A. Halbouni, T.S. Gunawan, M.H. Habaebi, M. Halbouni, M. Kartiwi and R. Ahmad. *Machine Learning and Deep Learning Approaches for CyberSecurity: A Review.* IEEE, vol. 10, pp. 19572–19585, 2022.
8. A. Guezzaz, S. Benkirane, M. Azrour, and S. Khurram. A reliable network intrusion detection approach using decision tree with enhanced data quality. *Security and Communication Networks*, vol. 2021, p. 1230593, 2021.
9. Y. Hamid, M. Sugumaran and L. Journaux. Machine learning techniques for intrusion detection: a comparative analysis. In *Proceedings of the International Conference on Informatics and Analytics* (pp. 1–6), 2016, August.
10. M. Maray and J. Shuja. Computation offloading in mobile cloud computing and mobile edge computing: Survey, taxonomy, and open issues. *Mobile Information Systems*, pp. 1–17, 2022.
11. M.M. Belal, D.M. Sundaram. Comprehensive review on intelligent security defenses in the cloud: Taxonomy, security issues, ML/DL techniques, challenges and future trends. *Journal of King Saud University: Computer and Information Sciences*, vol. 34, no. 10, pp. 9102–9131, 2022.

12. Z. Chiba, N. Abghour, K. Moussaid, A. El Omri and M. Rida. A cooperative and hybrid network intrusion detection framework in cloud computing based SNORT and optimized back propagation neural network. *Procedia Computer Science*, vol. 83, pp. 1200–1206, 2016.

13. A. Guezzaz, A. Asimi, Y. Asimi, M. Azrour, S. Benkirane. A distributed intrusion detection approach based on machine learning techniques for a cloud security. Intelligent systems in big data, semantic web and machine learning. *Advances in Intelligent Systems and Computing*, vol. 1344. pp. 85–94. Springer, 2021.

14. A. Guezzaz, A. Asimi, Y. Asimi, Z. Tbatou and Y. Sadqi. A lightweight neural classifier for intrusion detection. *General Letters in Mathematics*, vol. 2, no. 2, pp. 57–66, 2017.

15. A. Guezzaz, Y. Asimi, M. Azrour, and A. Asimi. Mathematical validation of proposed machine learning classifier for heterogeneous traffic and anomaly detection. *Big Data Mining and Analytics*, vol. 4, no. 1, pp. 18–24, 2021.

16. H. Attou, A. Guezzaz, S. Benkirane, M. Azrour, and Y. Farhaoui. Cloud-based intrusion detection approach using machine learning techniques. *Big Data Mining and Analytics*, vol. 6, no. 3, pp. 311–320, 2023.

17. M. Mohy-eddine, A. Guezzaz, S. Benkirane, et al. An effective intrusion detection approach based on ensemble learning for IIoT edge computing. *Journal of Computer Virology and Hacking Techniques*, pp. 1–13, 2022.

18. A. Guezzaz, M. Azrour, S. Benkirane, M. Mohy-eddine, H. Attou and M. Douiba. A lightweight hybrid intrusion detection framework using machine learning for edge-based IIoT security. *International Arab Journal of Information Technology*, vol. 19, no. 5, pp. 822–830, 2022.

19. M. Mohy-eddine, A. Guezzaz and S. Benkirane. An efficient network intrusion detection model for IoT security using K-NN classifier and feature selection. *Multimedia Tools and Applications*, pp. 1–19, 2023.

20. C. Hazman, A. Guezzaz, S. Benkirane, M. Azrour. IDS-SIoEL: Intrusion detection framework for IoT-based smart environments security using ensemble learning. *Cluster Computing*, pp. 1–15, 2022.

21. M. Douiba, S. Benkirane, A. Guezzaz, M. Azrour. An improved anomaly detection model for IoT security using decision tree and gradient boosting. *Journal of Supercomputing*, vol. 79, no. 3, pp. 3392–3411, 2023.

22. F. Jiang, Y. Fu, B. B. Gupta, Y. Liang, S. Rho, F. Lou, F. Meng, and Z. Tian. Deep learning based multi-channel intelligent attack detection for data security. *IEEE Transactions on Sustainable Computing*, vol. 5, no. 2, pp. 204–212, 2018.

CHAPTER 9

Design and Implementation of Intrusion Detection Model with Machine Learning Techniques for IoT Security

Mouaad Mohy-eddine, Kamal Bella, Azidine Guezzaz, Said Benkirane, and Mourade Azrour

9.1 INTRODUCTION

The emergence of information technology in many fields of human life has raised more security concerns [1]. Many technologies and programs have been developed to improve cyber-security and solve security concerns [2]. The IoT is the conjunction of billions of embedded sensors [3], providing a useful purpose [4]. Because of the rapid development of IoT technologies, the fundamental concept of IoT security is to maintain confidentiality, privacy, availability, and data [5]. The merging of diverse protocols and

DOI: 10.1201/9781003438779-9

data in the IoT makes using safety techniques in IoT frameworks increasingly challenging [5], [6]. Applying IoT security approaches is difficult due to the number of sensors, limited memory and processing capacity, and limited energy [7, 4]. Many solutions, such as antiviruses, firewalls, and intrusion detection systems (IDSs), have been implemented to protect systems from intrusion [8], [9], [10], [11]. IDS is designed to detect normal and abnormal system behavior based on signatures, rules, or behaviors [8]. It performs a key role in capturing disallowed uses and detecting modifications and destructions in the systems [9]. It attracted much attention because of its proven productivity and dependability [12]. Intrusion detection techniques are signature detection methods that compare the signatures database or patterns to the detected events to identify intrusions. The anomaly detection approach learns typical behavior and interprets deviation as an assault. The hybrid detection technique is a combination of signature and anomaly detection approaches that try to combine their benefits. Many recent papers [13] emphasize the significant benefits of data quality and machine learning (ML) approaches in increasing IDS performance. Furthermore, the limit of detecting zero-day assaults is gained by utilizing IDSs in conjunction with ML models [14]. This work seeks to design and evaluate a network IDS (NIDS) model for Internet of Things (IoT) security. To identify threats, the k-nearest neighbor (KNN) algorithm is applied to the Bot-IoT dataset. According to our observations, the method employed outperforms different approaches.

The rest of this paper is organized as follows: Section two provides an overview of IoT, IDS, and ML. We also offer relevant IDS works, notably those involving ML approaches. Section three displays our KNN-based NIDS and the feature selection method we applied. Section four contains experimental research that outlines how to implement proposed solutions. Following that, we look at the outcomes to see how successful our proposed model is. The conclusion and future work complete the paper.

9.2 BACKGROUND

There is no agreed-upon definition of what the things in the IoT might be [15], nor is there a standardized architecture, for there is no normalized architecture for the IoT [1], [4], [16]. As a result, numerous researchers have suggested alternative IoT architectures.

The most fundamental IoT architecture has three layers: application, network, and perception [4], [15]. The perception node for data collecting and control [7] is one of two components of the perception layer [1]. The control commands are carried out via the perception network. The core layer of the IoT is the network layer [1] which carries data from sensors and may also handle processing [17] and data security [7]. The availability of services [7] such as the smart grid, the smart environment [18], the healthcare system, and intelligent transportation, might influence how the application layer is constructed in various ways [3].

An attempt to automate [18], [20] and maintain the security system [14]is made by an IDS, which can be either a hardware or software system [19], [20]. IDSs can be used to increase system security with other security measures [21], such as access control, authentication systems, and encryption methods [22], It is thought of as a surveillance system 919]. IDSs scan the network and assess the collected packets against a database of known threats [21]. Additionally, it monitors the system and categorizes passing packets as intrusions or normal [10]. IDSs come in three different varieties: Signature based Intrusion Detection Systems (SIDS), Anomaly-based Intrusion Detection Systems (AIDS), and hybrid IDS (HIDS). SIDS matches the patterns or signatures to the discovered events [14], [8], [9], [19]. SIDS has been less effective as zero-day attacks have increased since no prior signature was kept for any new assaults. As a result, AIDS is viewed as a panacea. It can detect zero-day attacks by deducing typical activity patterns and classifying aberrant deviations as assaults [14], [8], [9], [19] SIDS and AIDS are combined in HIDS. The training step discovers the appropriate characteristics and classes, after which the algorithm learns from this data, and the testing phase applies the trained model to classify new data. ML approaches are either supervised or unsupervised learning [23]. Supervised learning [23] methods require labeled data to prepare a model. Some of the classification approaches used to create IDS include KNN [24], naïve Bayes (NB) [25], support vector machine (SVM) [8], [13], decision tree (DT) 26], random forest (RF) [27], and artificial neural network (ANN) [28]. The KNN [29] classifier is a non-parametric classifier that approximates the function locally and delays all calculations until the function is assessed. Using a labeled database, it can categorize data among its KNN. Unsupervised learning 23] approaches employ unlabeled data to train the model. Unsupervised learning approaches present in IDS works include K-means [30], density-based spatial clustering of application with noise (DBSCAN) [31], [32], and isolation forest (IF) [33, 34].

9.3 RELATED WORKS

In their study, Mohy-eddine et al. [35] describe an ensemble learning-based intrusion detection strategy for IoT networks. The RF classifier was implemented for the classification process. They combined IF and Pearson's correlation coefficient (PCC) for the feature selection phase. For evaluation, they used the Bot-IoT and NF-UNSW-NB15-v2 datasets. They investigated the impact of the applied order of the IF and PCC on intrusion detection by applying IF+PCC and PCC+IF, then compared it with IF only and PCC only. The model resulted in 99.98% and 99.99% accuracy (ACC) and 6.18s and 6.25s prediction time on Bot-IoT (IFPCC and PCCIF), respectively. The two models also scored 99.30% and 99.18% ACC and 6.71s and 6.87s prediction time on NF-UNSW-NB15-v2. Using the CICIDS2017 dataset, Ahmim et al. [36] created a HIDS incorporating tree-based approaches such as REP Tree, JRip method, and RF. The first uses dataset characteristics to assess whether each row is normal or intrusive. The second one works similarly to REP Tree, allowing you to choose the attack category. The final classifier uses the dataset attributes as inputs and outputs of the first and second models to recognize typical incursions. Using this hybrid method, they hope to discern the proper sort of captured assaults with a low False Alarm Rate (FAR) and a high Detection Rate (DR). According to Jie et Shan [8], data quality is crucial for enhancing IDS performance. Their suggested solution employed SVM and the NB feature transformation technique to produce new high-quality data from the original features. They build their model using the SVM classifier on the changed data. On diverse datasets, their experiment accuracies were 93.75% on UNSW-NB15, 98.92% on CICIDS2017, 99.35% on NSL-KDD, and 98.58% on KYOTO 2006+. Jie and Shan claim that their technique outperforms existing SVM-based algorithms in terms of ACC, FAR, and DR. Guezzaz et al. [37] present a network intrusion detection model based on DT and enhanced with data quality on the NSL-KDD and CICIDS2017 datasets. They compared their model to others that used the same data. Their model achieved 99.42% accuracy with the NSL-KDD dataset and 98.80% 3 with CICIDS2017. Meidan et al. [38] suggested a novel approach for detecting vulnerable IoT devices. They employed LGBM, DNN, and SVM. They plan to use the following performance indicators to assess their proposed model for the techniques above training time, classifier size, flow classification time, and area under the precision-recall curve (AUPRC). The LGBM took the shortest time to train, the SVM

TABLE 9.1 Summary of proposed models

References	Methods	Year	Datasets	Accuracy (%)
Jie and Shan [8]	SVM/NB	2020	UNSW-NB15	93.75
			CICIDS2017	98.92
			NSL-KDD	99.35
			KYOTO 2006+	98.58
Ahmim et al. [36]	REP Tree, JRip, and RF	2019	CICIDS2017	96.66
Guezzaz et al. [37]	DT	2020	CICIDS2017	98.80
			NSL-KDD	99.42
Meidan et al. [38]	LGBM DNN SVM	2021	CIDDS-001, UNSW-NB15, and NSL-KDD	Other metrics
Mohy-eddine et al. [35]	KNN	2023	Bot-IoT	99.99
Hazman et al. [39]	AdaBoost	2022	IoT-23	99.98
			Bot-IoT	99.99
			Edge-IIoT	100
Douiba et al. [40]	Catboost	2022	IoT-23	99.99
			Bot-IoT	99.99
			NSL-KDD	99.92

had the smallest classifier size, the SVM outperformed the other classifiers in the AUPRC, and the LGBM outperformed the different classifiers in the AUPRC. Hazman et al. [39] developed an intrusion detection framework for an intelligent environment security model. The model is based on an ensemble learning technique such as AdaBoost and combines different feature selection techniques such as Boruta, mutual information, and correlation. They evaluated their model on IoT-23, Bot-IoT, and edge-IIoT datasets, resulting in 99.98%, 99.99, and 100% ACC, respectively. Douiba et al. [40] designed an anomaly detection model based on catboost library to validate the developed model. They evaluate their model on NSL-KDD, Bot-IoT, and IoT-23 datasets. The approach resulted in 99.92% ACC on the NSL-KDD dataset, 99.99% on the Bot-IoT dataset, and 99.99% on the IoT-23 dataset (Table 9.1).

9.4 OUR APPROACH

We presented our technique based on the KNN model in detail in this section. The feature selection methods are applied to enhance data quality and save time.

9.4.1 Proposed Approach of the Schematic

Figure 9.1 depicts the components of our proposed architecture, which are characteristic of an IDS [8, 22]: data source module, pre-processing module, decision core module, and response module. In addition, the pre-processing portion received a lot of attention. We used feature selection algorithms to reduce training time and increase model performance.

We employed GA and PCA for the feature selection stage to save time, minimize computation costs, improve model performance, and aid in model convergence [41], [42]. Feature selection aims to locate the characteristics most relevant to the output while increasing data quality and conserving important information. This contributes to the development of an effective KNN model for NIDS.

9.4.2 Description of Solutions

We substituted string column values with numerical values to increase the classifier's performance and data quality. We deleted redundant columns, such as the textual presentation of the utilized protocols, while retaining the numerical presentation column. Unneeded columns were deleted, including category, subcategory, and incremental ID. We discovered some duplicate rows in the pre-processing portion as well. We propose applying feature selection algorithms to avoid the dataset's excessive dimensionality. Many feature selection algorithms have been developed to reduce the number of features before training. We employed PCA and GA to complete the feature selection method in this article. The PCA is a multivariate data analysis tool that attempts to minimize the size of a dataset while preserving important information. The GA selects the optimal set of features as a fitness function based on a combination of the most excellent Area Under the Curve – Receiver Operating Characteristic (AUR-ROC) score,

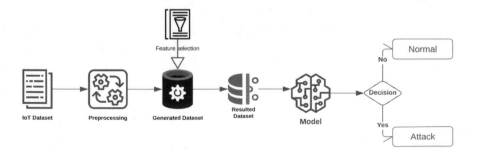

FIGURE 9.1   Proposed approach scheme

the highest ACC, and the lowest FPR. Using these tactics, we want to minimize training and testing time and computation costs and increase data quality and model performance. Using these strategies, we created datasets with the top ten performing features. We should use 10-fold cross-validation (CV) to validate our model. This technique aims to randomly choose nine chunks of the same size from the dataset to train the model and then test it. The 10-fold CV procedure does not waste much data since it repeats the operation ten times, resulting in a classifier that can identify fresh data and resists overfitting by utilizing earlier predictions as the new training data for the subsequent fold. We used the KNN classifier for classification, which assigns a label to each row. During the training and validation phases, the KNN gained classification capacity, correctly categorizing the cases.

9.5 EXPERIMENTAL STUDY

9.5.1 Dataset and Experiments Evaluation

The validation of intrusion detection systems is highly reliant on model assessment. A vast number of datasets are publicly accessible for testing ML-based IDSs. Our proposed model was trained, analyzed, and validated using the Bot-IoT dataset. It has lately gained popularity, notably in the IoT domains.

Koroniotis et al. [41] used a testbed, an environment designed to produce network traffic, to create the Bot-IoT dataset. The testbed was developed at the University of New South Wales Canberra's Research Cyber Range Lab. To make the dataset, they used five IoT scenarios [41]. With a total of 73.370.443 instances, the Bot-IoT dataset has 9.543 normal traffic and 73.360.900 attacks (Table 9.2).

Our experiments used a 2.30GHz Intel(R) Core(TM) i5-6200U CPU, 12GB DDR3 RAM, and Windows 10 Pro-x64-bit.

The performance of a classifier varies as its parameters are altered. As a result, we will use a grid research strategy to discover the best KNN classifier parameters for the dataset. Creating a grid of hyperparameter values and evaluating each combination in the grid provides an ensemble

TABLE 9.2   Bot-IoT dataset details

Normal instances	9.543
Attack instances	73.360.900
Total	73.370.443

of hyperparameters with high accuracy and low error. GridSearchCV is a hyperparameter optimization or tuning approach that produces a single set of high-performing hyperparameters for our model. Our primary aim is to decrease detection mistakes. Thus we developed and compared several feature selection algorithms, such as PCA and GA. We investigated the performance of KNN on our ten selected features, and the ten best features presented in [41].

6.5.2 Performance Metrics

In this study, we evaluated the classifier's performance using a variety of metrics (Table 9.3).

$$(1)\ \text{Accuracy}: \frac{TP + TN}{TP + TN + FP + FN}$$

$$(2)\ \text{Recall}: \frac{TP}{TP + FN}$$

$$(3)\ \text{Precision}: \frac{TP}{TP + FP}$$

$$(4)\ \text{F1-score}: 2 \times \frac{Precision \times Recall}{Precision + Recall}$$

$$(5)\ \text{AUC}: \int_{2}^{1}(TPR)d(FPR)$$

True positive (TP): is the number of correctly recognized attacks.

False positive (FP): is the number of incorrectly classified attacks.

True negative (TN): is the number of correctly recognized normal instances.

False negative (FN): is the number of incorrectly classified normal instances.

TABLE 9.3   Confusion matrix

		Actual Values	
		Attack	Normal
Predicted Values	Attack	TP	FP
	Normal	FN	TN

9.5.3 Discussion of Results

After applying our suggested feature selection to the dataset, we achieved the result presented in Table 9.4 , where we individually compared the performance of our classifier on PCA, 10-Best, and GA.

Table 9.4 compares the 2 proposed approaches with the 10 characteristics used in [41]. The study findings are practically comparable, with 99.99% accuracy for all techniques and 99.99% recall for all methods except KNN-PCA, which obtained 100%, 99.99% precision for all 3 approaches, and 99.99% F1-Score for all methods.

Figure 9.2 shows the impact of our model on the prediction time. We studied the prediction time of the three models, and the KNN-GA scored a superior result. The 10 best features scored 57.35 seconds, the KNN-PCA scored 580.23 seconds, and the KNN-GA scored the best prediction time with 51.89 seconds.

Our approaches produce excellent results and have excellent detection capabilities. In addition, Table 9.5 compares our model with several current systems based on the Bot-IoT dataset. Some ML approaches, including NB, C4.5, RF, and CNN, are used in the works listed in Table 9.5.

TABLE 9.4   Performance metrics of KNN-PCA, 10-Best, and KNN-GA

Model	Accuracy (%)	Recall (%)	Precision (%)	F1-Score (%)
KNN-PCA	99.99	100	99.99	99.99
10-Best	99.99	99.99	99.99	99.99
KNN-GA	99.99	99.99	99.99	99.99

TABLE 9.5   Comparison of our model with previous work on Bot-IoT dataset

	Method	Accuracy (%)	Recall	Precision
Ullah I. et al. [43]	CNN1Dim	99.96	0.99	0.99
	CNN2Dim	99.98	0.99	0.99
	CNN3Dim	99.98	0.99	0.99
Shafiq M. et al. [44]	RT	99.99	1	1
	Bayes Net	99.77	0.99	1
	C4.5	99.99	1	1
	NB	99.79	0.98	0.99
	RF	99.99	1	1
Our Approach	KNN-PCA	99.99	1	0.99
	10-Best	99.99	0.99	0.99
	KNN-GA	99.99	0.99	0.99

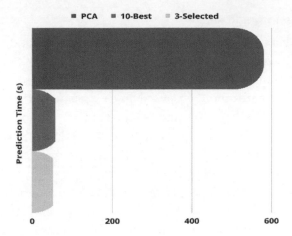

FIGURE 9.2 The evolution of the prediction time of the 10-Best, KNN-PCA, and KNN-GA

As indicated by the results obtained using the Bot-IoT dataset, our technique produces more convenient results than previously presented approaches. We were able to attain outstanding results for our model by utilizing feature selection approaches. However, the GA method used did not incorporate prediction as a parameter in the fitness function and therefore is unconcerned with the correlation or any other information in the features.

9.6 CONCLUSION AND FUTURE WORK

IDS has proven to be a vital tool for protecting hosts and networks since its inception. In this study, we developed an effective intrusion detection system based on KNN and feature selection methods. The data quality is critical for enhancing detection capabilities in the pre-processing portion. We suggested two feature selection algorithms, PCA and GA, to choose a subset of the entire dataset and then used KNN to evaluate the intrusion detection model. The results indicate that our method has the potential to produce good results, emphasizing the importance of feature selection approaches in boosting the effectiveness of intrusion detection systems. To summarize, compared to existing intrusion detection algorithms, our solution outperforms them.

REFERENCES

1. M. Azrour, J. Mabrouki, A. Guezzaz and Y. Farhaoui, "New enhanced authentication protocol for internet of things," *Big Data Mining and Analytics*, vol. 4, no. 1, pp. 1–9, 2021.

2. R. Von Solms and J. Van Niekerk, "From information security to cyber security," *Computers & Security*, vol. 38, pp. 97–102, 2013.

3. P. M. Chanal and M. S. Kakkasageri, "Security and privacy in IoT: A survey," *Wireless Personal Communications*, vol. 115, pp. 1667–1693, 2020.

4. P. Sethi and S. R. Sarangi, "Internet of Things: Architectures, protocols, and applications," *Journal of Electrical and Computer Engineering*, pp. 1–25, 2017.

5. M. B. Mohamed Noor and W. H. Hassan, "Current research on Internet of Things (IoT) security: A survey," *Computer networks*, vol. 148, pp. 283–294, 2018.

6. M. Azrour, J. Mabrouki, Y. Farhaoui and A. Guezzaz, "Security analysis of Nikooghadam et al.'s authentication protocol for cloud-IoT," In : *Intelligent systems in big data, semantic web and machine learning*. Cham : Springer International Publishing, pp. 261–269, 2021.

7. F. A. Alaba, M. Othman, I. A. T. Hashem and F. Alotaibi, "Internet of Things security: A survey," *Journal of Network and Computer Applications*, vol. 88, pp. 10–28, 2017.

8. J. Gu and S. Lu, "An effective intrusion detection approach using SVM with naïve Bayes feature embedding," *Computers & Security*, vol. 103, p. 102158, 2020.

9. A. L. Buczak and E. Guven, "A survey of data mining and machine learning methods for cyber security intrusion detection," *IEEE Communications Surveys & Tutorials*, vol. 18, no. 2, pp. 1153–1176, 2016.

10. A. Guezzaz, A. Asimi, Y. Asimi, Z. Tbatou and Y. Sadqi, "A lightweight neural classifier for intrusion detection," *General Letters in Mathematics*, vol. 2, pp. 57–66, 2017.

11. M. Mohy-eddine, S. Benkirane, A. Guezzaz and M. Azrour, "Random forest-based IDS for IIoT edge computing security using ensemble learning for dimensionality reduction," *International Journal of Embedded Systems*, vol. 15, no. 6, pp. 467–474, 2022.

12. A. Aldweesh, A. Derhab and A. Z. Emam, "Deep learning approaches for anomaly-based intrusion detection systems: A survey, taxonomy, and open issues," *Knowledge-Based Systems*, vol. 189, p. 105124, 2020.

13. J. Gu, L. Wang, H. Wang and S. Wang, "A novel approach to intrusion detection using SVM ensemble with feature augmentation," *Computers & Security*, vol. 86, pp. 53–62, 2019.

14. A. Khraisat, I. Gondal, P. Vamplew and J. Kamruzzaman, "Survey of intrusion detection system: Techniques, datasets and challenges," *Cybersecurity*, vol. 2, pp. 1–22, 2019.

15. S. A. Al-Qaseemi, H. A. Almulhim, M. F. Almulhim and S. R. Chaudhry, "IoT architecture challenges and issues: Lack of standardization," *2016 Future Technologies Conference (FTC)*, IEEE, pp. 731–738, 2016.

16. M. Azrour, J. Mabrouki, A. Guezzaz and A. Kanwal, "Internet of Things security: Challenges and key issues," *Security and Communication Networks*, vol. 2021, p. 11, 2021.

17. A. Tewari and B. B. Gupta, "Security, privacy and trust of different layers in Internet-of-Things (IoTs) framework," *Future generation computer systems*, vol. 108, pp. 909–920, 2020.

18. M. Mohy-eddine, A. Guezzaz, S. Benkirane and M. Azrour, "IoT-enabled smart agriculture: Security issues and applications," in *Artificial Intelligence and Smart Environment*, Springer International Publishing, 2023, pp. 566–571.

19. H.-J. Liao, C.-H. R. Lin, Y.-C. Lin and K.-Y. Tung, "Intrusion detection system: A comprehensive review," *Journal of Network and Computer Applications*, vol. 36, no. 1, pp. 16–24, 2013.

20. A. Guezzaz, A. Asimi, Y. Asimi, Z. Tbatous and Y. Sadqi, "A global intrusion detection system using Pcapsocks sniffer and multilayer perceptron classifier," *International Journal of Network Security*, vol. 21, pp. 438–450, May 2019.

21. A. Guezzaz, A. Asimi, Y. Asimi, M. Azrour and S. Benkirane, "A distributed intrusion detection approach based on machine leaning techniques for a cloud security,". In Intelligent Systems in Big Data, Semantic Web and Machine Learning (pp. 85-94). Cham: Springer International Publishing, pp. 85–94, 2021.

22. M. A. Ferrag, L. Maglaras, S. Moschoyiannis and H. Janicke, "Deep Learning for cyber security intrusion detection: Approaches, datasets, and comparative study," *Journal of Information Security and Applications*, vol. 50, p. 102419, 2020.

23. A. Guezzaz, Y. Asimi, M. Azrour and A. Asimi, "Mathematical validation of proposed machine learning classifier for heterogeneous traffic and anomaly detection," *Big Data Mining and Analytics*, vol. 4, no. 1, pp. 18–24, 2021.

24. M. Mohy-eddine, A. Guezzaz, S. Benkirane and M. Azrour, "An efficient network intrusion detection model for IoT security using K-NN classifier and feature selection," *Multimedia Tools and Applications*, vol. 82, pp. 1–19, 2023.

25. A. A. Sallam, M. N. Kabir, Y. M. Alginahi, A. Jamal and T. K. Esmeel, "IDS for improving DDoS attack recognition based on attack profiles and network traffic features," in *2020 16th IEEE International Colloquium on Signal Processing & Its Applications (CSPA)*, IEEE, 2020, pp. 255–260.

26. K. Peng, V. Leung, L. Zheng, S. Wang, C. Huang and T. Lin, "Intrusion detection system based on decision tree over big data in fog environment," *Wireless Communications and Mobile Computing*, vol. 2018, pp. 1–11, 2018.

27. M. Mohy-eddine, A. Guezzaz, S. Benkirane and M. Azrour, "An effective intrusion detection approach based on ensemble learning for IIoT edge computing," *Journal of Computer Virology and Hacking Techniques*, pp. 1–13, 2022.

28. J. O. Mebawondu, O. D. Alowolodu, J. O. Mebawondu and A. O. Adetunmbi, "Network intrusion detection system using supervised learning paradigm," *Scientific African*, vol. 9, p. e00497, 2020.

29. N. S. Altman, "An introduction to kernel and nearest-neighbor nonparametric regression," *The American Statistician*, vol. 46, pp. 175–185, 1992.

30. J. Chen, X. Qi, L. Chen, F. Chen and G. Cheng, "Quantum-inspired ant lion optimized hybrid k-means for cluster analysis and intrusion detection," *Knowledge-Based Systems*, vol. 203, p. 106167, 2020.

31. M. Ester, H.-P. Kriegel, J. Sander and X. Xu, "A density-based algorithm for discovering clusters in large spatial databases with noise," in *Kdd-96 Proceedings, Munich*, AAAI Press, 1996, pp. 226–231.

32. A. Saxena, K. Saxena and J. Goyal, "Hybrid technique based on dbscan for selection of improved features for intrusion detection system," in *Emerging Trends in Expert Applications and Security*, Springer, 2019, pp. 365–377.

33. F. T. Liu, K. M. Ting and Z.-H. Zhou, "Isolation forest," in *2008 Eighth IEEE International Conference on Data Mining*, IEEE, 2008, pp. 413–422.

34. K. Sadaf and J. Sultana, "Intrusion detection based on autoencoder and isolation forest in fog computing," *IEEE Access*, vol. 8, pp. 167059–167068, 2020.

35. M. Mohy-eddine, A. Guezzaz, S. Benkirane, M. Azrour and Y. Farhaoui, "An ensemble learning based intrusion detection model for industrial IoT security," *Big Data Mining and Analytics*, vol. 6, no. 3, pp. 273–287, 2023.

36. A. Ahmim, L. Maglaras, M. A. Ferrag, M. Derdour and H. Janicke, "A novel hierarchical intrusion detection system based on decision tree and rules-based models," in *2019 15th International Conference on Distributed Computing in Sensor Systems (DCOSS)*, IEEE, 2019, pp. 228–233.

37. A. Guezzaz, S. Benkirane, M. Azrour and S. Khurram, "A reliable network intrusion detection approach using decision tree with enhanced data quality," *Security and Communication Networks*, vol. 2021, pp. 1–8, 2021.

38. Y. Meidan, V. Sachidananda, H. Peng, R. Sagron, Y. Elovici and A. Shabtai, "A novel approach for detecting vulnerable IoT devices connected behind a home NAT," *Computers & Security*, vol. 97, p. 101968, 2020.

39. C. Hazman, A. Guezzaz, S. Benkirane and M. Azrour, "lIDS-SIoEL: Intrusion detection framework for IoT-based smart environments security using ensemble learning," *Cluster Computing*, pp. 1–15, 2022.

40. M. Douiba, S. Benkirane, A. Guezzaz and M. Azrour, "Anomaly detection model based on gradient boosting and decision tree for IoT environments security," *Journal of Reliable Intelligent Environments*, pp. 1–12, 2022.

41. N. Koroniotis, N. Moustafa, E. Sitnikova and B. Turnbull, "Towards the development of realistic botnet dataset in the Internet of Things for network forensic analytics: Bot-IoT dataset," *Future Generation Computer Systems*, vol. 100, pp. 779–796, 2019.

42. T. Kuang, Z. Hu and M. Xu, "A genetic optimization algorithm based on adaptative dimensionality reduction," *Mathematical Problems in Engineering*, vol. 2020, pp. 1–7, 2020.

43. I. Ullah and Q. H. Mahmoud, "Design and development of a deep learning-based model for anomaly detection in IoT networks," *IEEE Access*, vol. 9, pp. 103906–103926, 2021.

44. M. Shafiq, Z. Tian, Y. Sun, X. Du and M. Guizani, "Selection of effective machine learning algorithm and Bot-IoT attacks traffic identification for

internet of things in smart city," *Future Generation Computer Systems*, vol. 107, pp. 433–442, 2020.

45. R. Wazirali, "An improved intrusion detection system based on KNN hyperparameter tuning and cross-validation," *Arabian Journal for Science and Engineering*, vol. 45, no. 12, pp. 10859–10873, 2020.

46. S. Waskle, L. Parashar and U. Singh, "Intrusion detection system using PCA with random forest approach," in *2020 International Conference on Electronics and Sustainable Communication Systems (ICESC)*, IEEE, 2020, pp. 803–808.

Index

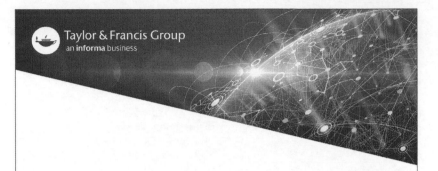